Cognitive Behavioral Therapy:

11 Powerful Steps to Freedom from Anxiety, Depression, Master Your Emotions, Say Goodbye to Negative Thoughts and Bring Up Positive Thoughts, Great to Listen in Car!

Table of Contents

Introduction......6

Chapter 1: "Cognitive" and "Behavioral" and 'Therapy"......10

Chapter 2: The CBT Model......18

Chapter 3: Getting to Know Your Thoughts......29

Chapter 4: Changing Your Own Mind......42

Chapter 5: Cognitive Distortions......54

Chapter 6: Core Beliefs......65

Chapter 7: Regulating Emotion......75

Chapter 8: Behavioral Activation, or just do it!......84

Chapter 9: Problem Solving Skills......92

Chapter 10: Mindfulness......100

Chapter 11: Radical Acceptance......109

Chapter 12: Improving Your Relationships with People......117

Chapter 13: Using Exposure to Counter Fear......129

Conclusion......137

Disclaimer

This book is the author's personal opinions about cognitive behavioral therapy. The author is not your healthcare provider or therapist. The author and publisher are presenting this book as information and not as health advice. Please consult your own physician or healthcare provider regarding any concerns about your mental or physical health.

© Copyright 2019 Tony Bennis - All rights reserved.

The following eBook is reproduced below with the goal of providing information that is as accurate and reliable as possible. Regardless, purchasing this eBook can be seen as consent to the fact that both the publisher and the author of this book are in no way experts on the topics discussed within and that any recommendations or suggestions that are made herein are for entertainment purposes only.
Professionals should be consulted as needed prior to undertaking any of the action endorsed herein.
This declaration is deemed fair and valid by both the American Bar Association and the Committee of Publishers Association and is legally binding throughout the United States.
Furthermore, the transmission, duplication, or reproduction of any of the following work including specific information will be considered an illegal act irrespective of if it is done electronically or in print. This extends to creating a secondary or tertiary copy of the work or a recorded copy and is only allowed with an expressed written consent from the Publisher. All additional rights reserved.
The information in the following pages is broadly considered to be a truthful and accurate account of facts and as such any inattention, use, or misuse of the information in question by the reader will render any resulting actions solely under their purview. There are no scenarios in which the publisher or the original author of this work can be in any fashion deemed liable for any hardship or damages that may befall them after undertaking information described herein.
Additionally, the information in the following pages is intended only for informational purposes and

should thus be thought of as universal. As befitting its nature, it is presented without assurance regarding its prolonged validity or interim quality. Trademarks that are mentioned are done without written consent and can in no way be considered an endorsement from the trademark holder.

Introduction

Congratulations on downloading *Cognitive Behavioral Therapy: Change Your Own Mind* and thank you for doing so.

The following chapters will discuss a variety of topics related to cognitive behavioral therapy from the perspective of someone who wants to help themselves and their mental health. Even if you are in overall good mental health, the techniques described here can help you be happier, healthier, and more effective. And if you *have* depression, anxiety, or other mental health issues, exploring cognitive behavioral therapy is the best choice you can make for your life.

Research shows that CBT is an effective intervention for a wide variety of mental health concerns (Dobson & Khatri, 2000; Hofmann, Asnaani, Vonk, Sawyer, & Fang, 2012; Tolin, 2010). CBT can help if you have problems with depressions, anxiety, relationships, or simply living life. It can help if you use too many substances or eat too much. You may struggle to make decisions about relationships, your career, or your life goals. You may be worried about the future or overly concerned with the past. You may simply be unhappy. CBT can help. CBT, in fact, is the type of therapeutic practice with the most empirical support.

Cognitive behavioral therapy was developed in the 1960s by Aaron T. Beck and Albert Ellis specifically for depression, but later researchers have adapted and used it for other conditions such as hypochondria, eating disorders, panic disorders, social phobias, and generalized anxiety disorder. Variants have been tested and found effective for borderline personality disorder, schizophrenia, bipolar disorder, obsessive-compulsive disorder, and posttraumatic stress disorder. As a model and a framework, CBT seems to help any maladaptive patterns or problematic mental health.

CBT is based on four fundamental principles, which we explore in more depth over the course of this book.

1. People's understanding about the world and the way they think influences how they feel and how they behave. This means that you can understand someone's problems through understanding the way that their thoughts, emotions, physical reactions, and behavior interact.

2. People can learn to become aware of their thoughts and, through the use of CBT interventions, can actually change those thoughts.

3. When a person changes their thoughts, their emotions, behaviors, and physical reactions will also change.

4. Because all these things are interrelated, changing your behavior will also change your thoughts and feelings.

The thing that that makes CBT so innovative and important is that it is a method of helping you feel better and adjust your emotions to be healthier by changing your thoughts and behaviors. It helps your feelings but does not directly deal with feelings, if that makes sense. It is not like the cliché of therapy where you are on a couch and telling an old man about how you feel about your mother. The focus isn't on your childhood or your deep feelings.

Instead, we are going to focus on what you *think* and what you *do*. By changing the way you think, you can change the way you feel. And, by manipulating your behavior, you can feel happier and more at peace with your life. CBT gives you the power to intervene directly to the core of the problem.

If you are disciplined and careful, you can do a lot of this work yourself. This book will help you develop the skills necessary to challenge your own thoughts and help change your own behavior. If you find that you need help, look into finding a therapist trained in CBT techniques for a couple of sessions. The nice thing about CBT is that it is not designed to be eternal therapy: it is a discrete, focused system with a specific number of sessions.

There are plenty of books on this subject on the market, thanks again for choosing this one! Every effort was made to ensure it is full of as much useful information as possible, please enjoy!

Works Cited

Dobson, K. S., & Khatri, N. (2000). Cognitive therapy: Looking backward, looking forward. Journal of Clinical Psychology, 56(7), 907-923.

Hofmann, S. G., Asnaani, A., Vonk, I. J., Sawyer, A. T., & Fang, A. (2012). The efficacy of cognitive behavioral therapy: a review of meta-analyses. Cognitive therapy and research, 36(5), 427-440.

Tolin, D. F. (2010). Is cognitive–behavioral therapy more effective than other therapies? A meta-analytic review. Clinical psychology review, 30(6), 710-720.

Chapter 1: "Cognitive" and "Behavioral" and "Therapy"

The secret to cognitive behavioral therapy is in the name – it is therapy that focuses on "cognition" and "behavior." This chapter will break down exactly what that means and contextualize CBT in terms of other therapeutic interventions. This will be helpful even if you don't have any previous knowledge or experience of therapy—you have an idea of what therapy should look like, even if only from TV, and it is useful to differentiate CBT from that conception.

"Cognitive therapies" treat behavior as mediated by thoughts. What you think determines what you do. Someone who is depressed has conscious thoughts that are negative and pessimistic these thoughts are possible to change. Early in the development of CBT, research was finding that people who had a "negative explanatory style" were more at risk for depression (Seligman &. Abramson, 1979). That is, people who see the worst in situations or always look for a pessimistic read on a situation are more likely to become depressed. Cognitive therapy works to change the way you interpret and think about situations in order to improve the way you feel. All cognitive therapies, including CBT, emphasize education and learning new skills that can be used to change your own mind.

There are three basic principles that all forms of cognitive therapy believe, and they are important to take seriously when learning about CBT.

First, there is principle that our thoughts are knowable. CBT is not focused on the subconscious or preconscious. This would be more in line with psychoanalysis, which believes that our behavior is determined by our subconscious mind. In psychoanalysis, the purpose of therapy is to draw out things that we do not consciously think but that affect our day to day lives. Cognitive therapies, on the other hand, endorse the idea that with appropriate training and attention, every person can become aware of their own thinking. You do not need a psychoanalyst to analyze the way your mind secretly works. The important thoughts are the conscious ones and the ones on the surface. This doesn't mean that the only thoughts that matter are surface ones about day to day things—your deepest beliefs are also important and will be discussed. The important thing is that the thoughts are accessible and conscious.

Second, there is the principle that our thoughts determine how we feel and what we do in response to various situations in which we find ourselves. It isn't the case that you simply act without thinking or just become overcome with emotion that you cannot control. The model holds that the way we think about an event is crucial in terms of how we feel. Emotions depend on judgments and judgments are about thinking. For example, you only feel anxious if you have the judgment that there is a threat or something to worry about in the situation. In order to have the emotion of anxiety, the judgment is also necessary. Many people feel like their emotions are automatic or beyond their control. We will talk about this in great depth later, but the important thing to note is that CBT doesn't think that is true. It only feels true because we get into a strong habit or routine of a particular emotional reaction. For instance, if we have the judgment that something is threatening, we start to develop in ourselves the habit of avoiding that thing. Eventually, we may become overcome with fear just seeing it, without having the conscious experience of thinking. However, even in those cases, where emotional and behavioral responses seem to be purely reflexive, CBT believes that there are thoughts that occur between the event and the person's responses to that event.

The third principles follow from the first two. Specifically, CBT holds that because we can know what we think and what we think controls how we react to specific situations, we can intentionally modify how we respond to the events around us. Using the skills that you learn in this book, you will be able to become more functional as you come to better understand the ways that your mind works. This means that there is no sense that anyone is "doomed" to a particular mental illness or maladaptive pattern of thought and behavior. Even though you might be diagnosed with a particular mental health concern, diagnosis is not destiny. You can change the way you act by changing the way you think.

In addition to these principles, there is another important assumption that says that an accurate view of the world is a healthy view of the world. Sometimes we have the social conception that optimists are delusional and that to be "realist" is to view things badly and negatively. CBT holds the opposite. The general idea is that when we better understand the real world or objective reality, we will become better adapted to deal with it. People are capable of becoming more in tune with the world around them and that when they are in tune, they will have better mental health. People who systematically perceive the world incorrectly, on the other hand, will often demonstrate behaviors that are not very adaptive. CBT holds that individuals who distort the world around them will have more problems.

Related to this, CBT is very concerned with whether or not thoughts are *useful*. Patterns of thinking come from long term experience with the world around us. Core beliefs, which we will talk about in great detail later, affect how we view the world and how we choose to interact with it. This means that our beliefs can, in fact, *limit* our opportunities, by changing the type of situations that we put ourselves in or by limiting the range of activities that we see as possible. That is to say, our thoughts can become self-fulfilling prophecies. Our core beliefs affect our future and the possibilities we see in it.

There are three broad types of cognitive therapies: those that focus on restructuring thoughts, those that focus on developing coping skills, and those that focus on solving problems. All of these types of therapies are examples of CBT and they are compatible with each other. The differences lie within the degree that the therapies focus on cognitive or behavioral change. Cognitive restructuring therapies are almost entirely focused on the way you think. They have the philosophy that emotional pain and maladaptive behavior is derived from disturbances in thinking. The goal, then, is to help you think more rationally and adaptively. Coping skills therapies, on the other hand, are specifically focused on developing a set of skills that help the individual in external situations that they find stressful. Thoughts are less specifically targeted, unless they negatively affect the person's ability to respond to a stressful event. Problem solving therapies have the goal to teach you a set of helpful strategies to deal with a variety of problematic situations and the strategies can either be cognitive or behavioral. This is between the two previous types of theory—neither entirely focused on behavior nor thoughts.

This book will cover the whole range of cognitive behavioral therapy. We will have examples of cognitive restructuring, coping skills, and problem solving. The goal is to help you learn to feel better in as many ways as possible. The goal is to help you find an approach that works for you. In order to do that, explore a wide variety of interventions and learn different skills. You will then be able to put them together in your own life.

All that is mostly about the "cognitive" in CBT, though we talked a little about behavior. What about the "behavioral?" Behavioral therapy derives from a theory of psychology known as "behaviorism," which says that the best way to understand human behavior is to look at the relationship between action and its consequences. One of the fathers of behaviorism, BF Skinner, called this "operant conditioning." Simply, operant conditioning depends on the rule that behavior that is reinforced tends to be repeated and behavior which is not reinforced tends to be weakened (Skinner, 1988). His famous experiment was putting rats in a "Skinner Box" where certain behaviors were either reinforced with treats or punished. He found that behaviors that were reinforced tended to be repeated and punished behaviors died out.

Behavioral determinations are focused on the specific behaviors that the whole person engages with. The goal in behavioral therapy, unlike many other therapies, is *not* to find a specific diagnosis. We don't really care about the collection of symptoms in terms of what mental health condition you could be said to have. Instead, the important concern is the nature of your problems and how those problems affect your life. It does not matter what overall "illness" those problems are related to. In a sense, it is about your *behavior* and not your *identity*.

Behavior is viewed as specific to contexts and the environment that you are in. Because it is not concerned with an overall categorization of your identity, there is no assumption that your behavior is related to general characteristics of you. Instead, behavior is viewed in specific contexts and related to a specific environment. This means that when you think about how to "get better," the goal is to change the behavior, not a more generalized change in your self-concept.

This means that it is important to be clear about what problems, in particular, bring you to CBT. Don't think of yourself as "someone with depression" or a general label like that. Instead, identify the specific problems and behaviors that cause you suffering. What would you like to change about the things you do on the day to day?

To generalize, behavioral therapy focuses on two types of problems: when you do a behavior too much and when you don't do it enough. Behavioral excesses are when a person displays a particular behavior that happens too frequently or too intensely. This behavior becomes a problem for the person doing it. Common versions of behavioral excesses are promiscuous sex, compulsive gambling, or very disruptive attention seeking behavior. Someone who struggles with anger and the negative impacts of angry outbursts would also have a behavior excess. Because behaviorism is based around the idea that behaviors that are reinforced become repeated, a behavioral excess is a sign that somehow this behavior is getting reinforced. For instance, for someone who tends toward angry outbursts, this behavior may be getting reinforced by them getting their way and withdrawal from people disagreeing with them. Even though the behavior on the whole causes negative outcomes, there is specific, targeted reinforcement that reinforces the behavior.

The other type of problematic behavior is behavior that is deficit. This is when a person does not demonstrate adequate flexibility when adjusting behaviors in different circumstances. They just don't know what to do when certain situations happen or they don't have the ability to react appropriately. This tends to happen when either these behaviors were never learned or, when the behaviors were previously used, they were met with negative consequences. As we learned with operant conditioning, when a particular behavior is met with punishment, people tend not to continue doing that behavior.

Another aspect of behavioral therapy is a focus on creating coping skills. Coping behaviors are about how a person responds to difficult situations. Many behaviors that become problematic started out as coping behaviors—you eat because it makes you feel good after a bad day. This often means that you end up deficient in how to appropriately respond to difficulties. Everyone has to deal with difficulties over the course of their life—the only question is how well you respond to it.

This book will talk about a variety of strategies, both cognitive and behavioral. The thing that will guide us throughout is the principle that you have the power to change the course of your life. Nothing is fated, and nobody is doomed. If you learn how to intervene into your thoughts and behaviors, your life can get a lot better.

Works Cited

Seligman, M. E., Abramson, L. Y., Semmel, A., & Von Baeyer, C. (1979). Depressive attributional style. Journal of abnormal psychology, 88(3), 242.

Skinner, B. F. (1988). The operant side of behavior therapy. Journal of behavior therapy and experimental psychiatry, 19(3), 171-179.

Chapter 2: The CBT Model

This chapter will introduce you to the basic way that CBT understands the individual's interaction with the world. This is crucial to understand, because all other interventions depend on this model. Without internalizing the basic relations, the other interventions will be much more difficult. In order to help us understand the concepts in this chapter, we will use the example of Joe. Joe is someone who struggles with his life, as it currently is, and this chapter will start to explain why.

CBT is based on a cognitive model where there is a connection between thoughts, emotions, behavior, and the physical body. Thoughts affect the way the brain works, therefore producing both emotional states and behavior. While medication can affect the way our mind works, research shows that therapy focusing on the thoughts can actually change the structure of the brain.

The way we think about the world has profound effects on how we experience it. If someone strapped you into a roller coaster and told you it was a torture device, likely your reaction to going on the big drop would be very different. If we think we are having fun, we will instead modify our anxiety reaction and it will become overall pleasant.

For CBT, problems in our lives are related to the inadequacy of our behavioral repertoires or disruptions in our thoughts. What a healthy, satisfying life is like is different for different people, but there can be some generalizations. Someone is well-functioning when they are active and regularly do things that they enjoy and give them a sense of being capable. They respond well to challenges and are resilient in the face of negative situations. They see the positive, hopeful side of things and have a generally healthy self-esteem.

For many of us, there are things that get in the way of that ideal. Sometimes, we have a deficient in behavior. Someone could have high levels of social anxiety and, in analysis, be found to have difficulty holding a conversation and is a poor listener. That person might need specific, focused skills in order to improve their life. Someone else who has social anxiety, however, could have the necessary skills, but still be anxious and avoidant of social situations because they believe that they are awkward. That person needs more cognitive intervention.

For most people, a combination of behavioral and cognitive tools is useful to dealing with the way that your problems manifest.

To go to our example, let's look at Joe's life. Joe is a loner and has always thought of himself that way. When people ask him to do things, he thinks: "people are feeling sorry for me." This makes him irritated and he turns them down. When he interacts with women in any way, he pays close attention for any sign of criticism of dislike. If she responds to anything he says with disagreement, he thinks "I blew it" and becomes sad and withdrawn.

For Joe, social situations are a source of anxiety. He does not get any pleasure from interacting with people. While many people would take an invitation from friends as a good thing, for Joe it is a reason to be upset. His thought, that people feel sorry for him, is shaping how he reacts to the event in the world.

Joe, if you asked him after a date with a woman, would say "I feel like a failure." But what's happening there is a confusion between a feeling and a thought. The feeling he is having is sadness. He is having the *thought* that he is a failure. The distinction is important, because conflating the two prevents us from seeing the real cause of our actions.

Joe would probably be a frustrating person to interact with, in many ways. His constant attention for criticism and dislike will likely have the effect of making him a more difficult person to interact with. His view, that he is socially inept, could be proven true just through his fear. His manner of thinking is causing him a great deal of problem.

In CBT, psychological problems are understood as problematic thoughts and disturbances in thinking. Psychologists divide the problems of thought into three categories. The first category is "automatic thoughts." These can be about the self, the world, other people, the future, or any number of things. Automatic thoughts are the thoughts that come to you without any prompting and without conscious effort. In depressed people, they are frequently negative. One feature of automatic thoughts is they are frequently untrue or at bet, only partly true. This contributes to the fact that they are the easiest type of thought problem to change. You can test your automatic thoughts to see if they are accurate about the world and often, the realization that they are not reduces their power.

Learning to identify automatic thoughts is a crucial strategy of feeling better. We will talk more about it in Chapter 3. Learning to sift through your own mind and isolate your thoughts is a crucial skill. Once you have determined what your thoughts are, you can start to change them, which we will discuss in great detail in chapter 4. You will learn to come up with alternative thoughts, determine if the thought is even true, and keep track of your emotional relation to the thought.

The goal of CBT is to help you reach a more accurate and logical conclusion about the world than your automatic thoughts provides. To return to Joe, it would be useful for him to evaluate the thought that his friends just feel sorry for him. If he looked at the evidence, he would probably find reason to think that they genuinely enjoyed spending time with him and that they were friends with him because of the positive things he added to their lives. If he evaluated the truth of his automatic thought, he would likely find out that it was false.

The second category of thought disruption are in the "rules" a person sets for themselves that lead to expectations that they have for themselves or for others. These are sometimes understood as "intermediate beliefs" and they can serve to protect you against negative outcomes. If you are generally convinced that you aren't a worthwhile person to be around, you might develop the "rule" that you should always work to please everyone so that they will deign to keep you around.

Joe, unfortunately, had a tough childhood. His mother was very hard on him and he learned to be ashamed of himself when he made any mistake. He developed the rule that "if you let people get close, they will be critical and reject you." This rule leads him to keep people at arm's length, because there is the risk that they will be mean if he let them too close.

This leads to the last category of thoughts, known as "core beliefs." These are the basic commitments that individuals have and typically, have thought for a long time. These are the basic beliefs that a person has about themselves, others, and the world in general. These core beliefs can be triggered by outside events and rise to the surface. In general, these beliefs are pretty inarticulate and vague. Most people don't have a very defined set of beliefs that they could write down. At the same time, they are often very rigid and learned early in life. These core beliefs are experienced as reality by a person who believes them, regardless of what the actual truth is.

Core beliefs often explains why people react very differently to events in their life. Divorce is very difficult for everyone, but if someone has the core belief that they are unlovable and worthless, it can be totally devastating.

Joe is talking to several people that he knows. He makes a remark about a TV show that they all watch. One woman, just after he makes the remark, looks away and waves to a friend across the room. Joe is super embarrassed, and he thinks, "she must think I'm an idiot." Because of these feelings, Joe leaves the group.

Joe sincerely believes that this woman thinks he is an idiot, but he doesn't have much evidence that is the case. What is driving the thought here is the underlying commitment to his own worthlessness and defectiveness. The actual events would not justify a hurt reaction—they only make sense in the context of the core belief.

It may feel to Joe that it is the actions of the woman that cause his behavior, but from the outside it is clear that isn't the case. It is the way he is thinking that is leading to the feelings. Further, leaving the group means that he is behaving in ways that make him socially more isolated and reinforce the problems he is having.

In general, any situation has five factors. It has thoughts, feelings, physical reaction, behavior, and the environment which affects all of those things.

To look at the specific example of Joe, we can break it down in the following way:

Situation: Woman waves across the room.

Joe's Thoughts: She thinks I'm an idiot.

Joe's Feelings: Depressed and worthless

Joe's Physical Reaction: Exhausted and stomach hurts.

Joe's Behavior: He gets up and leaves the group, curtailing a chance to deepen his social connections.

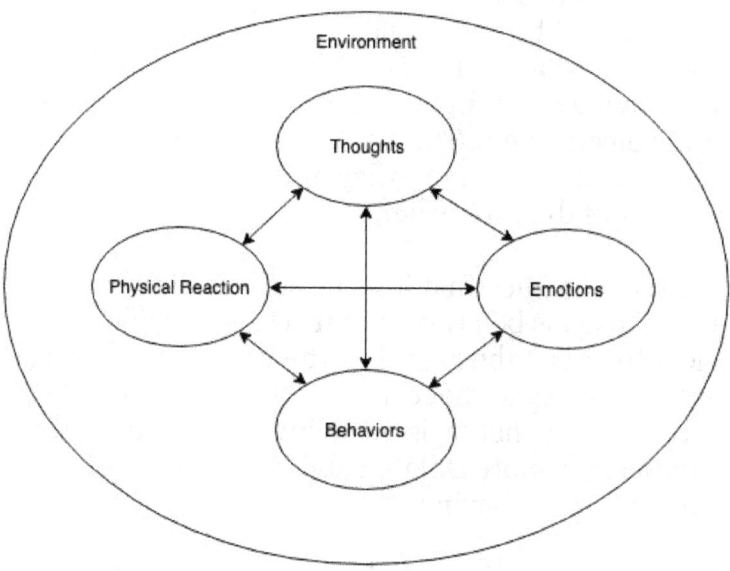

Fig 1 – Five part model to understand any situation.

If you look at the figure, you can see how a change in one factor can affect all the rest of the areas. Get into the habit of seperating all these parts from one another when you analyze a situation you are in.

"A situation" is whatever actually happened. It is the objective reality without interpretation. In Joe's case, it is the physical wave that the woman he was speaking to made. Anything else is extra. For instance, the fact that a child has a test coming up is a situation. The idea that it is a "hard test" is a situation plus the interpretation.

It is also important to be able to differentiate feelings and thoughts in order to fully use this model. We often confuse thoughts and feelings in our speech. I might say "I feel like he doesn't like me," but what is actually meant is "I think that he doesn't like me." Be careful not to conflate them that way. Feelings tend to be one word such as mad, happy, worried, sad, anxious, excited, and so on. Thoughts tend to be more developed and come in the form of sentences or phrases.

We have lots and lots of thoughts, especially automatic ones. Many of our automatic thoughts are no problem at all. When I go to the grocery store, I might have the automatic thought "where is my shopping list?" That is fine and likely causes me no emotional distress. The automatic thought, though, that "I am stupid," will likely cause a great deal of distress. Our thoughts often come and go quickly, making it sometimes difficult to notice them. But when we have automatic thoughts that cause us distress, it is crucial to establish what our thoughts are.

Another important thing to differentiate is between feelings and physical reactions. Strong feelings are often accompanied by physical reactions, such as sweating, tingling, or tension. When you feel anxious, your muscles might go tight and your heart rate speeds up. It is important to separate them in part because people have different physical reactions to feelings. Sometimes, also, we can be having a strong physical reaction that we do not notice. And, further, sometimes we can feel better by handling the physical reaction as opposed to directly dealing with the feeling.

Behavior, the last of the four main factors, is what you actually do. The goal is to separate the behavior from the things that contribute to the behavior.

As you think about your life and the things that you struggle with, be careful to keep all of these things straight. Get in the habit of identifying thoughts, feelings, physical reactions, and behaviors as separate parts of a situation. When you think of a situation, take a moment to think about it without any thoughts or interpretation—just look at the situation.

Once you have sorted out the different aspect of your reaction, it is crucial to figure out then what is maintaining your problems. What is leading to the trouble that brings you to this book or to the idea of therapy?

As discussed, our thoughts drive our behavior. When we have different thoughts, we have very different feelings, physical reactions, and behavior. The way that we shape our thoughts can change the things that actually happen. Let's look at Susan and Kathy's thoughts and see how they respond to the same situation. Both Susan and Kathy are going to a work conference where they won't know anyone.

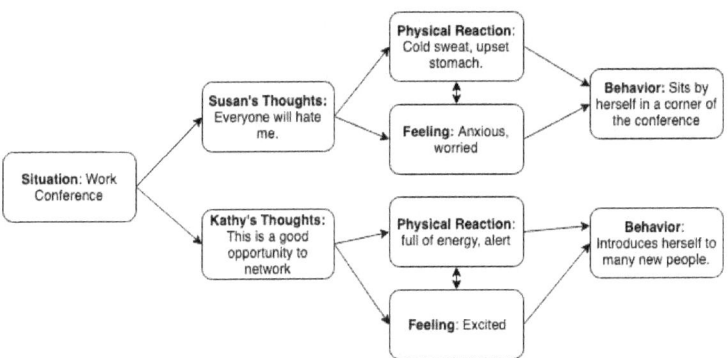

The work conference ends up going very differently for Susan and Kathy. For Susan, she is dreading this conference. She is worried about how she is going to deal with not knowing anybody and is convinced that people won't like or respect her. She thinks it is going to be brutal and alienating. This results in a variety of physical reactions and the feelings of anxiety and worry. As a result, she avoids other people over the course of the conference and ends up having a very alienating time. She feels like nobody likes her, because she did not end up talking to anybody.

Kathy, on the other hand, views the work conference as an opportunity to network and meet new people. For her, it is an opportunity that she does not know anyone. That means there are all sorts of new people to meet! Her emotions while thinking about the conference are excited and she is full of energy. This means she is eager to introduce herself to new people and ends up having a great time, full of conversation. This leads to very different experiences.

With Susan, we can see the way that problematic thoughts can reinforce themselves. She has the thought that the conference isn't going to well, which means she is anxious, which makes the conference not go well. There is a loop of behavior, thoughts, and feelings.

This also demonstrates why CBT is not just cognitive therapy, it also is *behavioral* therapy. With Susan, we can see directly how her behaviors are having an effect on her problems. It is her behavior of going to sit by herself that means nobody talks to her. Her behavior leads to the consequence of loneliness and alienation, which then is taken as evidence for the thoughts that the conference wasn't going to go well. There is a cycle that reinforces itself. If you are having trouble changing your thoughts, another type of intervention is to directly change your behaviors and that will help immensely.

The whole cycle presents different opportunities to intervene. For some people, intervening on the level of physical reactions can be very helpful. If someone is feeling very unpleasant, then taking a warm bath or doing something soothing can help change the emotion.

Chapter 3: Getting to Know Your Thoughts

A crucial first step in helping you change your own mind is getting to know what thoughts are running through your head and to get more familiar with how you react to problematic situations. Many of us are locked into automatic, negative paths. Something happens, and then the thoughts, feelings, and behaviors cascade over one another in an inevitable sort of way.

Careful self-analysis is critical in order to be able to "pause" this process and analyze what is going on. Using the four factors we discussed in the previous chapter, we can dissect our automatic responses and start to develop strategies to address our own problems.

People who have depression often have what is known as the "cognitive triad." This is the set of three negative views that characterize depression: negative views about yourself, negative views about the world, and negative views about the future.

It is useful to look for any of these negative thought patterns in your life. The first part of the cognitive triad, negative views about yourself, are somewhat easy to recognize. These are the automatic thoughts that include the personal pronouns *I, me,* or *my.* You might find yourself saying things like this:

- I am a bad person.

- Nobody likes me.
- I am terrible at my job.

As an exercise, take some time to write down the thoughts that you repeatedly have that are negative about yourself. What is the way that you beat yourself up? How do you speak to yourself when a mistake happens? These negative statements are global and seem to come automatically. Do not take time to evaluate whether or not the statements are true. Simply write them down.

The second element of the cognitive triad are views that are related to the world at large. These are sometimes more difficult to spot, because many people mistakenly think their negative views are just accurate descriptions of the world. Many people with thought disturbances have a vague sense that it is the rest of the world that is disturbed and only they are seeing things accurately.

A good clue that it is a negative outlook as opposed to an accurate description of the world is that it is absolute: if you think something *never* works out or *always* is bad, you probably are over-stating the case.

Either way, take some time to write down negative thoughts you have about the world. Do not evaluate whether or not the statements are true, at this point, just look for thoughts which are negative and directed outward. Some examples include:

- All men are jerks.
- The powerful are corrupt

- Life is unfair.

The last part of the negative cognitive triad are the negative thoughts that you have about the future. You might say to yourself:

- My life will get worse.
- Nothing will work out.
- The world is going to destroy itself.

These thoughts are predictions about how things are going to turn out and they are generally negative. Without stopping to determine whether or not they are true, write down all the thoughts you have about the future that are negative. Do you focus on the fact things will be bad? Are you continually predicting negative results for things that you might try?

Look at your lists. To what extent are you generally negative? In what category are your thoughts the most negative? It is crucial that you have a good sense of how your negative thoughts manifest and where you should focus your time.

Many people come to therapy with a general knowledge that they are gloomy, worried, or cynical. But, on the other hand, your thoughts feel true and accurate. You aren't pessimist, you might think, you are a *realist*. Evaluating all your negative thoughts as a collective is one way to come to the realization that there is a general pattern of negative thoughts.

The act of thinking about your thoughts is a skill in itself and it needs to be developed. Sometimes it will be difficult for people to establish the ability to analyze their thoughts.

Take one of the negative thoughts that you wrote about in the previous section and think of a situation where that negative thought arose. Did you find yourself thinking that nothing will turn out well of that your future was doomed? Describe that situation to yourself. It is often helpful to journal about it, describing what happened, how you felt, and what you did about it.

What effect did the negative thought have? Did it change your behavior in any way? Could you imagine your behavior changing if you had a different thought?

Make a worksheet with five columns: Situation, Feelings, Physical Reactions, Behaviors, Thoughts.

With the situation you are thinking of, fill out each of the columns. In the situation category, write down what happened. What happened? Who was involved? Where did it happen? When did it happen? In the "Feelings" column, write down what you felt and rank the intensity of that emotion from 1-10. In "Physical Reactions," write down how your body reacted and also rank that from 1-10. In "Behaviors," write down the actions that you did. Finally, in "Thoughts," write down the thoughts that you had in that situation.

Try to analyze what the relationship between these columns is and how they interacted with each other. As you go through your life, try to develop the habit of viewing things from the outside and analyzing them in this way.

It might be helpful to fill out this form every day. Make a point to spend time analyzing your situations and behavior so that you start to develop an awareness of patterns.

Every person has specific types of situations that set their automatic negative paths in motion. You have *triggers*—things that spur you on into the thoughts, feelings, and behaviors that lead you. to wanting to change. In order to address your problems, you have to know what type of situations are difficult for you and trigger your negative patterns.

Sometimes you will already be aware of your triggers. But for other people, it is difficult to identify the specific situations that provoke problematic emotions. You might think that you are "always" sad or "always" drink too much and be unable to identify specific situations that become problems

A helpful first step can be to monitor the problematic feelings or behaviors and see if there are some situations where the feelings are worse or the behaviors more problematic. Imagine someone who thinks she is "always angry." At first, this person might think they are angry all the time. But if she carefully monitored her feelings and determined when they were the strongest, she will begin to see patterns. Perhaps, in this particular case, she gets most angry at her teenage daughter when she doesn't do her homework or breaks curfew. She might find that her anger toward her daughter was overflowing into the rest of her life.

You can use a simple monitoring worksheet like the one below. When you use it, note what situations are the most difficult and rate your feelings from 1-10. When you do that, you will often start to see patterns. Imagine Richard, who feels like he is unhappy at his new school all the time. If he filled out the worksheet, it might look something like this.

What is your Trigger?	
Situation	Feelings (ranked from 1-10)
Monday: nobody to eat with at lunch	Unhappy: 10
Tuesday: in homeroom, the two other people sitting at my table talked to each other and not me.	Unhappy: 9
Wednesday: I overheard someone talking about a party they were having and they didn't invite me	Unhappy: 10
Thursday: a teacher invited another student to try out for the school play and didn't ask me	Unhappy: 8
Friday: I hung out alone at recess.	Unhappy 10

When Richard looks at the worksheet, all filled out like that, he can discover that he was the most unhappy in social situations. He was not listing unhappiness when he was in class or answering questions. He was only unhappy when he felt like he was excluded socially. It helped him realize that academically, school was going well. And maybe he was in band, and he didn't feel unhappy in band.

That could be going well. The problem was when he felt socially rejected.

Situations can involve interpersonal events, solitary things, or even things that are imagined. They can be memories, partial images, or mental pictures to which you are responding. They are often locked into certain times of day, so make sure to ask yourself questions about contextual aspects of the situation.

As you are trying to identify situations, ask yourself W questions. What happened? Who was involved? Where did it happen? When did it happen? It is in some ways similar to being a journalist, trying to figure out the facts of the matter. You need to have a sense of exactly what events caused the negative feelings or behaviors you are trying to target.

Sometimes, if you are struggling to figure out what is important about a particular situation, try describing the situation in vivid detail. Events exist in multiple senses, including sounds, smells, and touch. When you use multiple sensations, you can help yourself visualize the space you occupied and identify the sights, sounds, and sensations to help yourself trigger your memory. If the situation involved another person, you could ask trusted confident to roleplay the situation with you. They can take the place of the other person and then you can analyze the situation again.

One common thing that happens is that the situation that causes negative feelings and thoughts is not just one discrete situation or a single moment. Situations that trigger us can evolve over time. A dispute with a friend can start as a fairly minor insult or hurt and then quickly escalate into mutual insults, before you leave hurt and wounded. Your thoughts and feelings will likely evolve throughout the entire interaction. In those cases, it is useful to break the set of events down into specific moments with various stages of the interaction.

Always try to be as specific and concrete as possible when describing these situations to yourself. When you identify trigger situations in vague terms, you won't really get a full sense of what happened. Instead of saying "my wife does not respect my work," it would be better to say, "my wife told me that she thought her work was more important than mine."

When you get more specific and concrete, you move forward in the process of describing the world without interpretation. Sometimes our thoughts color what our memories are. In the previous example, your wife telling you she thought her work was more important. But what if she had said that she does not want to miss a work event for her company in order to attend a work event for yours? It is possible to remember this interaction as her thinking her work is more important. But on closer analysis of that thought, it is not justified by the situation. Her being unwilling to *prioritize* your work over hers does not mean she thinks that your work is unimportant.

One way to think of this is that the facts of a situation are different than the meaning of a situation. The goal is to separate the facts from the thoughts and feelings about the situation. An example might be is that you might describe your child as being very rude to her teacher. "Rude" is an adjective and describes what you *think* about your child's actions, but it does not describe what your child did. What exactly was the action?

Do not record situations with your thoughts and feelings embedded in them. Instead of thinking "I was so angry at my mother when she was late," separate those two elements. Your mother was late, and you were angry. The event happened, without the feelings, and then the feelings happened.

Sometimes it is difficult to identify your feelings. Feelings are one-word descriptions of emotions. Sometimes we might think we are feeling angry, but on closer analysis, actually be anxious or scared.

It can be helpful to just look at a list of feelings when you are troubled and see if any of them resonate.

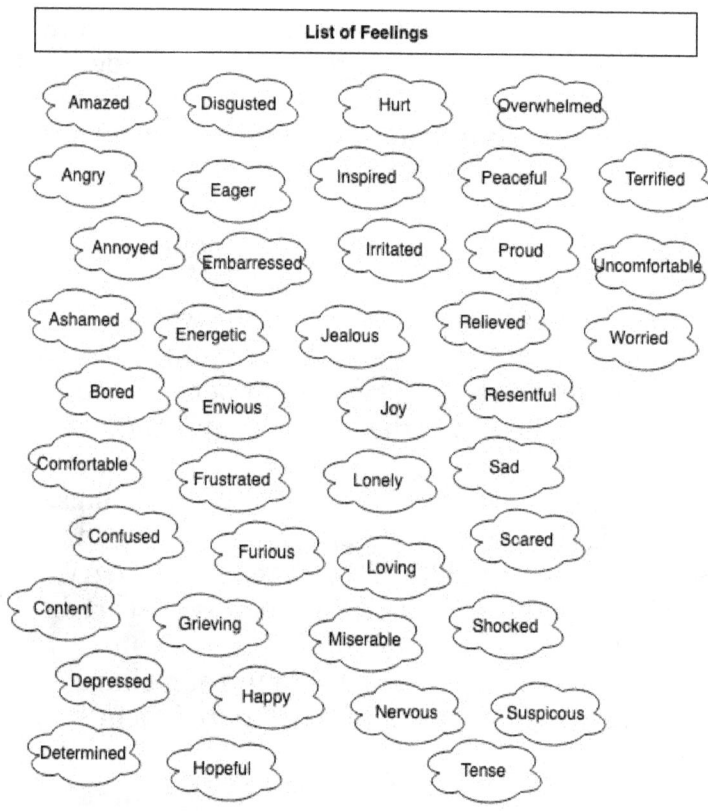

If you find yourself struggling to identify how you feel, look at this list and write down which ones resonate. Once you start to pay attention to your feelings, it will become easier and easier to label them. Some people have never asked themselves the question "what am I feeling."

Pay special mind to when you are physically tense or upset and try to label your feelings in that moment.

Sometimes it is difficult to identify our feelings because we have a tendency to identify thoughts as feelings. We might say "I feel stupid," but what you actually mean is that "I think I. am stupid" and correspondingly "I feel upset." Thoughts are very closely connected to feelings, but we need to learn to separate them.

After you are good at identifying your feelings, the next agenda item is identifying your behaviors. Ask yourself, what did you do? You are looking for behaviors that avoid the situation, are impulsive, or are likely to make the situation worse. Sometimes we minimize our behavior but slowing down and carefully analyzing what you did is important. You might describe what you did after getting angry at a friend as "letting off some steam," but when your face the facts squarely what you actually did was punch a wall and break your hand.

Sometimes we describe our behaviors as "giving up" or "freaking out," but try to be more specific when you describe your behavior.

The intervening element, between the event and the feelings and behaviors, is the thoughts. Remember our CBT model from before. Events happen in the world, we have thoughts about them, and those thoughts cause feelings and behaviors. After you have a sense of what events cause negative emotions and behaviors, the next step is to start to identify the problematic thoughts you have about those events.

Some thoughts are known as *hot thoughts*, because they carry an emotion and are strongly connected to intense feeling. We have some thoughts which are simply about the world and are basic facts or judgments. Some other thoughts, however, evoke an intense feeling. Hot thoughts can be things like. "My father never appreciates what I do for him" or "I always screw up." These thoughts are the ones you should to pay close attention to you.

As you look over the situations you've discovered that lead to problematic emotions or behaviors, think hard and evaluate what exactly the thoughts were that lead to the emotion. For instance, maybe you became very angry when a work colleague did not reply to an email quickly. The situation was "24 hours without a reply to this email." The feeling was "anger." Maybe the behavior that you did was "write a snarky follow up email." What was the thought that contributed to that feeling and behavior? Perhaps it was something like "not replying to my emails is disrespecting me." And, correspondingly, "the appropriate response to disrespect is anger."

Learning to analyze situations in the detail that we have used in this chapter is crucial for being able to separate our thoughts from the situation, the feeling, and the behavior.

As you learn to identify your thoughts, it can be helpful to use a daily record of thoughts. Some people print out worksheets, but others just like having a notebook where they can record what you are thinking. When you know what your thoughts are, you can start to push back against them.

The following structure may be helpful:

Situation (date, time, event.)	Thoughts about the situation	Feelings (list name and rate intensity 1-10)	Behaviors or actions

The information collected in this record is crucial. Once you know what you are thinking and how that effects your actions, you can start to change it.

Chapter 4: Changing Your Own Mind

The previous chapter was a discussion of how to identify problematic situations and the thoughts, feelings, and behaviors that come from them. If you have fully engaged in the process of self-analysis, you will likely have lots and lots of thoughts. How do you choose which thoughts to focus on changing?

- Look for thoughts that cause you intense emotional reactions. If the thought makes you feel furious or full of despair, that is an important thought to work with.
- Look for thoughts associated with strong patterns of behavior. Maybe every time you thought something in particular you drank too much. Or maybe whenever you think "I am not good in social situations," you left the party.
- Look for thoughts associated with your primary problems. For example, if you struggle with an eating disorder, look f or thoughts related to eating, food, and your body.
- Look for thoughts that are intensely or strongly negative. Thoughts in the "cognitive triad" we discussed in the previous chapter are super relevant there.

After collecting these thoughts, make a choice about which one to start with. It will likely be too difficult to work on combatting all your problematic thoughts at once, so it is best to pick a focus initially.

Once you have identified a target thought, you are going to work to change it. This chapter talks about two ways to intervene against a thought that is causing you problems. First, you can evaluate the empirical evidence for the thought and determine if it is fully true. Second, you can look for alternative thoughts and other ways to think about a situation.

Different thoughts will best be addressed in different ways. I'd suggest that you read and process this entire chapter, but. If you find that one of the methods of intervention doesn't seem to apply, that is okay. Sometimes you may evaluate the evidence for a problematic thought and determine that it is true. In that case, you should move on to the other styles of intervention.

Evidence-based Interventions

The first intervention we are going to talk about are "evidence-based interventions." These are mostly successful when you find that your thinking about a topic is distorted or overly negative. This occurs when you have somehow misperceived how the world "really" is. Sometimes we interpret the world to fit existing beliefs about ourselves or about the world and fail to see what actually happened.
This model of thinking about thoughts assumes that our perceptions of events are based on two sources. First, there are the actual facts of the situation in which we find ourselves. Second, we have a set of beliefs, assumptions, and schemas which help us interpret those facts. It is the interaction between

the real world and our inner beliefs that lead to our specific thoughts in individual situations. These core beliefs are themselves something we are going to talk about addressing in Chapter 6.

The next chapter will run through a list of cognitive distortions and talk about each one individually, so this chapter will be more general. We are going to talk about the overall strategy of assessing cognitive distortions.

A primary problem is that our thoughts generally *feel* correct. Nobody thinks things and simultaneously thinks those things are false. The very premise of believing something is that you believe it to be true. An important realization to come to is that just because something feels true, it doesn't mean it is true. It. Is just a thought.

Everything we say about the world is just a probability and we can think wrong things about the world. It is important to recognize that thoughts can be false. It is crucial to remain open to the idea that your thoughts may not be the gospel truth about the world.

Thoughts can be evaluated against the data of your experience. You have a whole life time of experience that you can use to determine if thoughts are true. You can even come up with experiments to test your thoughts, if you are unsure about them.

It is often useful to write down your evaluation of the thought. You could use a worksheet that is structured like this:

EXAMINE THE REALITY OF YOUR THOUGHTS	
Thought I want to examine:	
Evidence for My Thought	Evidence against My Thought
Conclusion or thoughts that consider all the evidence:	

Because you tend to assume your thoughts are true, using a worksheet like this to analyze the evidence can help start a process of self-reflection. You want to find balanced thoughts that more accurately reflects the world and the evidence around you.

Just one case of looking for evidence of a thought will not lead to total change. You need to complete this process many times, over many versions of similar problematic automatic thoughts, before you start to see systematic change in your thinking patterns. At the same time, because most people have recurring negative thinking patterns, focusing on one thought record will help the entire pattern.

A reality of the situation is that you will have some evidence for your problematic thoughts. You think these things for a reason, even if the reasons are somewhat exaggerated. Some people find it very helpful to write down this evidence. When it is in black and white in front of you, it can feel much more approachable. It is a fact that you can talk about, as opposed to something nebulous and scary. Often when you write down the negative evidence, you find that there is not nearly as much of it as you think there is. And, when you find out that the negative thoughts are fairly accurate, that is a chance to problem solve and try to find a behavioral fix to a situation.

It is important to be diligent about questioning yourself to reveal evidence that refused the original negative thought. It is easier to support your thoughts than try to disprove them. Make it almost a challenge to yourself or a game to try to think of as much evidence against your thought as possible.

Remember, evidence needs to be concrete and detailed. When you evaluate evidence for and against a negative automatic thought, it is similar to weighing evidence on a scale. On one side is the evidence for the thought and the other side is evidence against. Because we are more focused on the negative, the evidence for the negative thought tends to be very heavy and full of details. We remember in exact, vivid, and painful detail what we have done wrong. Often, the evidence against a painful thought will be vaguer and more abstract. The more you can specify detailed examples of evidence, the more you will be emotionally engaged and the more you believe the evidence against the thought.

If you have the thought that you are bad at making friends, you might have emotional and vivid examples of times that your attempts to reach out failed. Maybe when you invited four people to dinner, none of them said yes. That is easy to remember and feels like very strong evidence. On the other hand, when you think of evidence against this thought, you might just have the vague thought that you have "some friends." Ask yourself questions to make that evidence more compelling.

What are examples of some of your friends? What are your friends like? What sort of thing did you do with your friends? How did you know they wanted to be friends?

By asking these questions, you fill in details. You may discover that you genuinely have two or three good friends that you often see on weekends and get together with your children to play. Maybe you have been too stressed to reach out, recently. Maybe they've even reached out to you and it has felt too hard to say yes.

Sometimes it will be the case that you find you do not have enough evidence to make a conclusion at all. This is a useful situation, because it means you do not have the evidence to believe the negative thought. Why believe something that causes you pain if there is no reason to believe it?

This is a useful situation to gather more evidence, as well. Ask people you trust about their perspective on your thought. If you think that nobody respects your work, ask a coworker that you are close to for an honest opinion. Ask your boss for an evaluation. Find out the information you need to know whether or not the problem is in your thinking or your behavior.

Many people not only distort past events, but also predict negative futures. People who struggle with anxiety particularly focus on negative outcomes. As we learned in Chapter 2, you can even make the negative outcomes a reality through focusing too hard on them. Our negative expectations can become self-fulfilling prophecies.

Much in the same way you evaluate the evidence of a thought about the past or present, you can evaluate the truth of a prediction. Write down what you expect to happen and then specifically clarify what you would take as evidence to confirm or disconfirm their prediction. Ask yourself what the worst-case outcome is, the best possible outcome, and the most realistic outcome. What evidence would fit each situation?

Identify how you will collect the relevant evidence for the situation. Create a plan to evaluate your expectations. If necessary, come up with a way to record that evidence. Use the facts about the world to temper your negative expectations about the world.

As you think about the future, sometimes the reality is that you will not know what will happen. It is important to learn to tolerate uncertainty. The negative outcomes you fear are likely *possible*, but they are not certain. The fact they are possible must be accepted, even if it is scary. But possibility is not certainty, and it is not useful to be overwhelmed by fear.

In general, sometimes it will be easier to argue against a negative thought if you try to depersonalize it. Ask yourself questions like these:
- What would you say to someone else who thought this way?
- What do you think someone who cared for you would say if they knew you had this thought?
- If you felt better, what would you think?
- Five years from now, what might you think?

These types of questions can help you find evidence that you are otherwise inclined to ignore.

Alternative Thoughts

Evidence-based strategies are often effective, but they do not work when. The original thought was distorted. Sometimes, the original thought is negative and leads to emotional distress, but it may not be distorted. Sometimes negative thoughts are accurate. Bad things do indeed happen to good people. Sometimes, also, there is a distortion of some type, but it is useful to pair the evidence-based intervention with other types of strategy.

Sometimes when you review the evidence related to a negative thought, you will find that the thought s unhelpful. The evidence may not be clearly negative, but it is clear that the thought isn't doing you any good. In this situation, it is often useful to try and generate different and more adaptive thoughts. These thoughts will hopefully be more helpful, more caring, and more compassionate.

There is little value in replacing a negative distortion with a positive distortion, so it is important that this thought is accurate. But as you are brainstorming possible alternatives, focus on what the alternatives are before you spend time evaluating them. It is easy to get caught up in nitpicking and not be able to think of other possibilities.

Think of what thoughts are more helpful and more compassionate. Remember, you are a worthy person and deserve happiness in your life. What thoughts are more consistent with that fact? In general, let yourself imagine what a happy person would think about the situation or what a good person would think. Project positivity and from that perspective, imagine what you could think about the situation.

Once you have a list of possibilities, consider the advantages disadvantages of different ways of thinking about the situation. The negative thought has been causing you pain—that is a disadvantage. Does it have any advantages? Does the happier, more positive thought have any disadvantages? Carefully consider what the benefits to your life would be if you adopted the positive thought.

Let's say you have the thought that you aren't good at making friends. That thought has some evidence—maybe you don't have as many friends as you would like, and you can think of specific instances in which you have failed to make friends. There is, of course, some evidence against it—you have some friends and you were capable of meeting them. Either way, if you look at the effects of that thought, it can be illustrative. This thought contributes to sadness, that has a negative effect. It also leads to you withdrawing from social situations and opportunities to engage with new people. In that way, it can become a self-fulfilling prophecy.

If you chose to believe that it is possible for you to make new friends, you might feel less sad. That would be one benefit. It would also mean that you would be more likely to put yourself into situations where you interact with strangers in friendly ways. It would very likely result in more friendships. And you don't have think anything unrealistic—you don't have to imagine that you are incredibly extroverted and gregarious. All you have to accept is that it is *possible* that you can make new friends.

You will find, in close analysis, many thoughts that have this structure. Putting an alternative, more positive spin on your automatic thoughts may greatly increase your happiness.

Some people struggle to generate happy or positive alternative thoughts. If you are in this situation, one option would be to brainstorm with a loved one or someone who has your best interests at heart. They might be able to help you figure out alternative ways of looking at your life. You could even survey friends about the thought, to figure out what they think. If you think of a certain neighborhood as unsafe, maybe you could ask people about time they've spent in that neighborhood.

If your thoughts have a strong moralistic or religious character about what is right and wrong, try speaking with a clergy member or a trusted religious advisor. Often, they are very used to helping their followers work through complicated issues of morality and learn to be happier with themselves.

If you struggle to accept alternative thoughts, even when you know they would be better and healthier for you, try imagining yourself speaking to a child. What would you tell a child that is feeling the way you are feeling? How would you advise them to adjust their thoughts? This strategy can be helpful because often we are kinder and more compassionate to others than we are to ourselves. If you do not find the idea of talking to a child compelling, imagine talking to a friend that came to you with an echo of your thoughts. How would you advise them to adjust their thinking?

One strategy you can use with alternate thoughts is called TIC-TOC, an acronym that refers to the ticking sound of a clock. TIC-TOC stands for "task-interfering cognitions-task-orienting cognitions." The idea is to pair a frequent negative thought that interferes with your life with a positive thought that you can repetitively bring in to counter the negative thought. Maybe you find yourself continually thinking "I can't do it" when you are faced with certain types of tasks. If you develop a credible, quick alternative thought, you can train yourself to follow the negative thought with a positive one. An example could be "every little bit helps" or "I don't have to do it all right now." The goal is to have the alternative learn to be supplied automatically, every time you think the negative thought.

So, if you think "I can't do it," you will start to automatically reply "Every little bit helps." Using a short, catchy alternative to counter your short, catchy negative thought is a great strategy.

Chapter 5: Cognitive Distortions

In the process of weighing your own cognitive distortions, it is often useful to have a sense of what common types of cognitive distortions are. These errors in thinking are particularly prone to making symptoms of things like depression and anxiety worse, but all people occasionally fall into cognitive distortion. The important thing is to be able to recognize when you are making a mistake and correct it.

This chapter is going to go through a list of different cognitive distortions. Not all of them will resonate with you—most of us are more prone to some cognitive distortions over others. When you find one that seems familiar, make careful note of it. You want to learn to be able to spot it in your own thinking and push back against the error.

Jumping to Conclusions

In general, the cognitive distortion of jumping to conclusions is about reaching a conclusion without sufficient evidence. Instead of carefully and reasonably evaluating all the inputs, you instead go right to a particular conclusion. Usually that conclusion is negative and means bad things about your life. This causes a lot of pain.

One version of this distortion is known as "**mind reading**." This is the belief that we can tell what other people is thinking. Of course, it is possible to have evidence from behavior and physical posture about what people are thinking, but we often over-extrapolate and reach too-specific conclusions. For instance, we might see a stranger make an unpleasant face and conclude that she is thinking something negative about you. That would be an instance of jumping to conclusions. We do not have the evidence to know what she is thinking and yet, you make conclusions anyway.

Fortune telling is another type of jumping to conclusion. This manifests as the tendency to make predictions based on little information and holding to them as inevitable. One example would be to say that it is impossible for you to find love, because you haven't found it yet. It is fortune telling when you see one possible outcome as the only possibility, as opposed to one among many.

Personalization

This distortion involves taking everything and everyone personally. The distortion functions by making yourself the cause of all things around you. You might assume that if someone is moody, it is because they are irritated with you. Or, if your team didn't win the game, it is your fault.

This distortion involves making you the center of the universe. It is natural, in many ways, to do that. We are the most important person to ourselves. But it can be a freeing realization to focus on the fact that others don't think about us nearly as much as they think they do. Mostly people are concerned with themselves.

Attributional Bias

One type of cognitive distortion is an "attributional bias." Attributions are how we explain the causes of events. There are three elements of attribution: locus (internal vs external), stability (single occurrence/stable vs permanent/stable), and specificity (specific to one situation vs. global.). Locus is about whether or not you think events are caused by features about yourself or features in the outside world. Stability is whether or not you think the causes of events are permanent or if it is a particular, single occurrence. Specificity is similar but is more about whether this cause is only about one part of your life or your whole existence.

Research has shown that depression is related to the tendency to make internal, stable, and global attributions for failure. That is, when something goes wrong, someone with depression assumes that the fault is within themselves in such a way that will never change and will affect all parts of their life. At the same time, depressed people make external, unstable, and specific attributions for success. If they succeed, it was lucky and doesn't mean anything about the future.

People with anger problems have a different structure. They tend to make external, stable, and global attributions for negative outcomes. They might think, "he meant to insult me, and he will do it again." This is a reason for the outwardly directed emotion of anger.

Sometimes when you examine the attributions of events, you will find that you are using other cognitive distortions. You might be *mind reading* –

that is, assuming that you know the inner life of other people and why they are acting. You also might be personalizing—which is to say, interpreting events as being entirely about you.

Sometimes it is useful to actually make a chart, in order to test how you are attributing causal outcomes. Someone might think "my wife left me because I was such a bad husband," thereby attributing 100% of the blame to himself. But if you draw a pie chart and really consider it, you might find that there are other causes. Probably the wife had some effect on the relationship's failure, especially since she made a choice to leave. Maybe, if you consider the situation, you could assign her 30% of the responsibility. And maybe, on consideration, her extended family hated you and did not support the relationship. Maybe they get 10% of the responsibility. And maybe you had a large amount of work-related stress and travel, as well as finances. Give 10% to each of those factors.

If you look at it with those factors included, you might only have 40% of the responsibility for the situation. It is still useful to take responsibility, but it is not useful to blame yourself when the facts do not support that.

Overgeneralization

This is a version of the attribution bias. This distortion is when you take one instance and generalize it to a whole pattern. If you receive one bad grade, you extrapolate from that you will always receive bad grades and that you are a bad student.

The biggest problem with this type of cognitive distortion is that it is not very rational thinking. Inference, or the process of coming up with generalizable conclusions from specific situations, is one of the most difficult things that humans do. It is very hard to generalize about the whole world based on specifics. When you do so, you are most likely wrong.

Even worse than coming up with a bad prediction, your over-generalization may become a self-fulfilling prophecy. If you believe you are a bad student in general, you may not try as hard because it is painful to confront your failure. Then, you will do worse than you otherwise would.

Control Fallacies

These distortions are when you have misidentified the locus of control in some way, making them a variety of attribution bias. Control fallacies manifest either by thinking that we have no control over our lives and are totally victims of fate or by thinking that we are in complete control of ourselves and our surroundings, meaning we are totally responsible for everything. Both are incorrect. The truth is somewhere in between. We have some amount of control over our lives and we are also in some sense subject to randomness. Even in situations where you feel totally out of control, you do have choices about your mentality and internal approach to the situation.

Labeling

A common cognitive distortion is the assignment of a label. Labels are problematic because they feel permanent and make any change feel impossible. People can run into. Issues labeling themselves as well as other people. When you analyze the labels in your life, you will find that they often become self-fulfilling prophecies. If you label your boss as mean, you will interpret his behavior as mean.

It is important to recognize that people are complicated, and you do not know anybody, not even yourself, well-enough to label them overall. They can always surprise you and do something you did not expect. New events might reveal new facets of your own skills and personality.

When you make an overall label like "mean" or "stupid," you are ignoring the possibility of new evidence. Often, when it is a negative label applied to yourself, you may be ignoring evidence in order to speak badly of yourself. Use the skills we discussed in the last chapter to assess the truth of the label and whether you have enough evidence to speak absolutely.

All-or-nothing thinking

This is a very common cognitive distortion that a lot of peoples struggle with. It can involve an extreme attributional bias (something is *all* my fault), but it. Can also extreme judgments about a range of things. For example, someone might think "it was the *worst* I ever felt," or "I am a *total* failure," or "he is the *most* difficult person in the world."

Often, instead of expressing a trend or a tendency, we express an absolute. We use categorical terms. We might say "my boss is *totally* useless." The word "totally" is a clue that you are responding with all-or-nothing thinking. People mostly vary in how useful they are, and usefulness might improve over time with skill. If you find yourself thinking something this absolute, it is often a good idea to evaluate how you came to this judgment.

It is often useful to explore the continuum of possibilities. Imagine different spots on a scale and how someone might be more or less useful. You can even design little experiments to test the validity of the original thought—maybe you ask your boss for something that is in line with what you know of his expertise. This helps encourage a greater range of thoughts and a more evidence-based style.

Sometimes, when you are using the all-or-nothing thinking you are trying to express some underlying truth. For instance, the boss might not be "totally useless," but he might be not a good boss. He might be making your job unnecessarily difficult. You might want to look for a better job! The benefit of moving toward less all-or-nothing thinking is not that you are always wrong about your assessment, but that the absolute judgment is rarely consistent with the evidence. You want to try to be less dramatic and more evidence-based in your thoughts.

Emotional Reasoning

Emotional reasoning is a type of cognitive distortion when you assume that your feelings validate the thoughts that you are having. You think things are true because you feel something. For instance, you might think "My mother wanted to punish me; I felt so guilty." But, when you think about it, the reason why you think that your mother wanted to punish you is your feeling of being guilty.

You might feel guilty for a number of reasons, some of which might actually be related to your mother's behavior, but the emotional state of guilt cannot itself be a reason why the cause is true. This is a logical error. The effect of something cannot be determined just because something follows it.

It is important explore the actual situation. To what extent is your feeling explained by the behavior of your mother as opposed to your internal thoughts about that behavior. You could explore other reasons why your mother might have taken that behavior. Other than to make you feel guilty. There needs to be an evaluation of the evidence and data-gathering to determine the truth. Just because you feel very strongly, it does not make it true.

Mental Filter

This cognitive distortion involves focusing on the negative. Sometimes we get caught up in specific negative parts of a situation and don't evaluate all the evidence evenly. This can manifest by looking at a specific situation and extrapolating it to the entire relationship, for instance. It can also manifest by disqualifying the positive aspects of the situation.

If you receive a positive review at work, you might discount it by attributing it to your boss simply being too nice. This is particularly problematic version, because it means that you will not be able to see positive evidence.

Magnification or Minimization

These cognitive distortions are about exaggerating the importance or meaning of things or, alternately, minimizing the importance of things. Magnification is otherwise known as "catastrophizing." This is common in people with anxiety. Something happens, and instead of being considered in context, it is taken as the worst thing in the world and a total disaster.

Should Statements

A particularly damaging distortion is focusing on should statements. Should statements are when you tell yourself you "should" do something, or you "must" do something, or you "ought" do something. They can also be imposed on others, creating strong and probably unreachable expectations.

Holding on tightly to what "should" happen often results in guilt when we cannot meet our goals. With regards to others, thinking too strongly about what they "should" do will lead to anger and resentment.

Fallacy of Fairness

This fallacy is related to the "should statements," in that it is also concerned with what "should" happen. Instead of applying should statements to other people, in this case you apply it to the world. You might think, the world *should be* fair. The reality is that it is not, however.
If you judge all circumstances by whether or not it is fair, you will likely spend much of your life angry, resentful, and hopeless. You will inevitably be in many situations which are profoundly unfair.

Fallacy of Change

This distortion involves the idea that we can change others if only we act correctly. This is the idea that if only I did something right, then the other person will change their behavior. The reality is, only the individual can change themselves. Your behavior has very little to do with the choices they make about. their own lives. Falling into this fallacy can both be very frustrating and also lead to problems in your relationship with the other person, as you pressure them to change on your terms.

Always being right

This cognitive distortion comes from the idea that it is entirely unacceptable to be wrong or incorrect. If you have the belief you must always be right, correct, or accurate, the possibility of failure is horrifying and may lead to fervent fights to be proven right. This is problematic, because it could very well lead to doubling down on a failed endeavor and other negative behaviors. In general, it is also a distortion because nobody's worth depends on being right all the time. There is nothing wrong in being wrong and all people occasionally make a mistake.

Chapter 6: Core Beliefs

Core beliefs are part of how we interact with the world. A key part of the cognitive model is that our behaviors and feelings are a combined effect of the situation around us and our beliefs about the world and about ourselves. That means that while there are some critical life skills that can help solve problems that arise, there are also important core beliefs which lead control how we respond to situations.

One method for determining what core beliefs you have is known as the "downward arrow." In this method, you take an individual example of a negative thought and think to yourself, so what if it was true? What is the meaning of this thought being true? If you ask yourself what the implication of that fact is, you will have another belief. And then you can ask yourself, what the implication of that is. This can go on and on until you. reach a broad and irrevocable conclusion, which doesn't have any other place to go.

An example of this could be the evaluation of the thought "I am going to look like a fool if I speak in class." If you accept that is true, that you would look like a fool if you speak, what might that mean? One thing is that it could mean that your incompetence would be clear to everyone and that you would be embarrassed. And then you ask yourself, what does that mean? Perhaps you think that if everyone knew how incompetent you were, you should leave the class and go do something else. And then you ask yourself, what would that mean? Finally, you say that if you had to leave school, you would just crumple up and die. From that, there is no further meaning. That is the final thought.

This process can lead to a dark place. You should be careful when asking yourself these questions and try to remember that each of these steps aren't unequivocally true. But asking the questions allows you to do identify core beliefs, which are broad, stable, and core aspects of your way of thinking. Our surface thoughts reflect our core beliefs and we have many automatic thoughts that are caused by our core beliefs.

If core beliefs are so fundamental, why did we wait until chapter 6 to talk about them? Core beliefs are mostly productively addressed after there has been work dealing with more surface thoughts or automatic thoughts. Core beliefs can be distressing to work with and for some people, unnecessary. Some people can be helped just by thinking about their automatic thoughts. But for many people with systematic mental health struggles, if they don't address the core beliefs, there will be a relapse.

Core beliefs have several aspects including attitudes, values, assumptions, beliefs, and schemas. Attitudes and values are essentially long-standing opinions about a topic, with some emotional aspect. We can have positive or negative attitudes and attitudes are often about devaluing certain people, ideas, or objects.

Assumptions are long-standing opinions about the relationships between various concepts or people.

We might assume, for instance, that bad people will have bad karma and bad things will happen to them. You might also think, for instance, that you are unlovable and that nobody will ever care about you. These statements are essentially "if, then" statements. You have an assumption about the way the world is put together and then you have a related assumption about the implications of that belief.

Beliefs and schemas are reasonably stable ideas about objects, people, and concepts. They are likely formed as part of your development into an adult. Many things go into a child's set of beliefs about the world, including parents, the media, friends, and school. As children grow and develop, their personal experience will reinforce certain ideas that have been communicated to them. Over time, these ideas will coalesce into a belief or schema.

These beliefs can be categorical ("all women are flighty") or relational ("attractive people only fall in love with attractive people."). They can be directed toward the self, others, and the world in general. They can be historical and specific – "I was a happy child"—or future-oriented and general. ("I will never succeed"). Within cultures, there tends to be shared sets of beliefs. People have to learn the initial core of their beliefs from somewhere, and it tends to be from the world around you.

While there are differences between these different varieties of core belief, we are going to use the term core belief to refer to all of them. Core beliefs are how we process new information and organize existing information. That means they affect our memory and perception alike. We tend to ignore information that does not mesh well with our core beliefs. This bias is part of the reason why these beliefs are so durable: we cease to notice information that contradicts them.

All people have core beliefs. They only become a problem when they lead to feelings or behaviors that are causing suffering. When you find that you have similarities in the recurring thoughts that cause painful behaviors or feelings, there is very likely a core belief at the base of them.

One person might have a tendency call themselves "stupid." Another person might respond to every challenge by saying that it is "impossible." In order to be able to recognize and grapple with patterns like this, it is crucial to engage in the type of self-analysis discussed in chapters 3-5.

One clue that you are close to a core belief is if you have the strong sense that a current experience relates to an earlier experience in life. Recurrent experiences that are felt as similar are a good indication that you have a core belief that relates to both experiences. If you get dumped by a romantic partner and it feels similar to your parents getting a divorce, there might be a core belief that is coloring both of those situations for you. Listen carefully to the content of your thoughts, any feelings that these thoughts evoke, and the behaviors that you do in response to them.

Another way to test your own core beliefs is to imagine hypothetical situations and think about how you would respond to those situations. If you hypothesize certain types of relationship or action, you probably will be able to come up with a pretty good sense of how you will react. Sometimes imagining hypothetical situations can be a good precursor to actually trying them out. If you imagine how you would react to attending a new and unfamiliar church and work through your reaction, it might be possible to actually *do it* and see what happens.

Sometimes it is useful to think back into your past to evaluate where your core beliefs come from. Core beliefs typically form because they are in some sense *useful*, even though they are dysfunctional in a larger sense. Core beliefs serve some purpose in relating you to your environment. For example, if you were bullied as a teenager, you might develop the core belief that you are somehow weird or abnormal. That would at least explain the bullying behavior and is, in a sense, adaptive at that time. But later in life, that core belief could cause damage.

Once you have a clear sense of what core beliefs that you are working with, then you need to start the process of changing them. Engage in this with caution—changing core beliefs is much more difficult than directly addressing automatic thoughts.

Intervening with core beliefs begins with identifying the existing core-beliefs and then contrasting them with a preferred "new" core belief which is to replace them. This means that a crucial element is having a clear sense of what new belief should replace the old one.

One strategy used in changing core beliefs is to shift core beliefs from being general to being more specific. Someone could have the core belief of mistrusting others. This belief may have formed from many life experiences, including disengaged parents, social rejection, or even abusive relationships. But mistrust might now lead to things like rejecting social approaches from other people, fear of others, and wondering constantly about other people's motivations. Rather than trying to address the overall belief of mistrust, it may be easier to identify the key markers of the belief and change those. Instead of trying to be generally trustful, you could try to shift what causes you to feel mistrust.

Core beliefs tend to be held very strongly and in terms of broad categories. Common core beliefs are things like "I am totally worthless" or "women cannot be trusted." With such strong beliefs like this, sometimes it is difficult to find evidence against the belief. If something is held that strongly, evidence is hard to see. In that case, it is likely helpful to discuss whether or not things can be that strongly held in general. Is it possible that anybody would be *totally* worthless? Is there really no woman on earth that is trustworthy? Shaking the conviction that the core belief is *always* true will help you start to see alternatives and possible ways to shake the belief.

One way to reinforce shifts in core beliefs is about identifying key markers of the new core belief in practice. If you want to adopt a core belief of being friendly and open to people, it is useful to think about what behaviors, thoughts, and feelings go along with that core belief. Then, once you have a sense of what supports the belief, you can start to keep track of your actions that are in line with the belief that you want to foster. This shifts your focus toward evidence that is positive and keeps your gaze on your goal. Instead of focusing on what is negative, you can learn to focus on the positive. This can give you incentive to keep working on developing the new core belief.

As your core beliefs start to change, you want to start recording evidence for each of core beliefs that you are dealing with. Initially, you might find evidence that supports the dominance of your old belief system, but as change starts to happen, evidence for the new system becomes more believable. As you continue to grow and change, the relative strength of belief in the old core belief can be contrasted with the strength in the new core belief, allowing you to see shifts in your mindset.

It is useful to think about what types of evidence would cause you to change your mind about your core beliefs. Often, we feel our old core beliefs very strongly and it seems almost impossible to imagine change. Starting to ask yourself what could persuade you to change your mind would be helpful because it will start to prime you to see evidence that you might not have seen before.

Try not to set the standard for evidence so high that it won't ever be achieved. If you have unrealistic standards of evidence, you will be stymied in your project of changing your core belief. But at the same time, don't hold yourself to impossible standards of change. If you have spent your whole life thinking that everyone is out to get you, expecting yourself to morph into being trusting and calm with everyone you meet is likely to get you discouraged. You may start to prematurely perceive yourself as failing to change your mind. A more realistic alternative might be to learn to give people a chance before mistrusting them. Or, you could start to look for specific signs that someone is trustworthy or untrustworthy. The establishment of realistic standards makes movement toward new core beliefs much more possible.

One way to develop facility with new core beliefs is simple practice. For example, if your old core belief was that you are incompetent, and the new core belief is that you are self-assured and competent, you can help establish this by practicing acting with assurance and competence. Find situations where you can pretend to be self-assured, even though it might feel tacked on and artificial at first. Put yourself in situations where you can succeed and learn what it feels like to be self-assured. The principle of "fake it until you make it" can often work quite well. Just the simple act of pretending like you actualize your new core beliefs can often make it much easier to live them.

One way to think of this strategy is to. set up behavioral experiments. Figure out how someone who believes your new core belief would act and then try to act like that, just to see what it would feel like. Attempt to do what the new core belief would ask you to do and then evaluate how it feels, what the results are, and whether or not it helps your life in the way that you think it will.

For example, someone with the core belief that they will fail at anything they try will behave differently than someone with the core belief that they have a chance at success. If you pretended to believe that you could succeed, how might you act? What might you try to do? If you actually do those things, you might find that good things come about from the experiment. The direct experience of acting consistent with the core belief helps you learn to change your own mind about what to believe.

While we called this strategy "fake it until you make it" previously, a better way of thinking about it would be "do it until you feel it." When you do something, you start to set up patterns which will eventually trickle up into your mindset. Think of all the ways that your desired core belief might change your life and just start to do those things, regardless of whether or not it feels sincere. As you continue to do them, you will start to feel more and more authentically connected to your actions.

Spend some detailed time imagining the way that you would act if you believed the new core belief. One way to do this is to ask yourself questions about areas of your life where you are dissatisfied and want to change. Sometimes it is even useful to explore other people's stories about change in order to see that it is possible to radically restructure your life. Read a biography of someone you admire and learn how they shaped their life to the way they wanted it to be.

Sometimes, when you radically change the way you interact with the world, you will get pushback from the people around you. Some people might comment or even react negatively to positive changes in your life. This is useful evidence for who is truly supportive of you and who wants the best for you. Do not give in to social pressure and go back to your old ways-- that would be giving in to the old core belief.

Find people that support the way you want your life to look. It is important to have social support, but sometimes we find that our social environments are not conducive to the changes we want to make. Finding people who are consistent with your new goals can be a healthy and beneficial way to encourage yourself to change.

One way that can help you make the shifts in core belief that you need to make is to look into your past and determine the history of the belief's emergence. Why do you think what you think about the world? Trace your early experiences and evaluate what about them lead to your current set of beliefs. This often can help you gain purchase on your own feelings and emotions.

Chapter 7: Regulating Emotion

Sometimes we will have strong emotions. This is an inevitable result of being human. Many of the cognitive interventions that we have discussed in previous chapters can help mediate the intensity of negative emotions, but they won't always be enough. This chapter will talk about dealing with intense emotions and learning how to avoid negative behaviors in response to emotion.

One major feature in emotional regulation is learning to tolerate distress. Sometimes horrible things happen, and you feel horrible. Sometimes you cannot change the conditions you are in and you need to learn how to survive.

The core of distress tolerance is learning to use skills to make yourself feel better that are healthy and beneficial to you. Often when we are in distress or feeling intense emotions, we engage in behaviors that are not beneficial and that have the potential to hurt us. These can be directly as harmful as suicidal behavior or self-harm, or harmful in a more indirect way like over-eating and using substances.
Learning how to care for yourself in a healthy way is an important part of dealing with distressing emotions.

Most people already have the ability to distract themselves from harmful things, but most of us don't distract ourselves in healthy way. The goal is to find behavior that effectively distracts you from harmful emotions and yet, at the same time, doesn't cause any other problems for you. The goal is not to totally avoid your emotions and problems, but rather, to give yourself the ability to escape the harmful emotions when you need to.

Calming down from Crisis: TIPP

When you feel at an emotional breaking point and totally overwhelmed, the most important thing is to figure out how to bring yourself back away from the metaphorical ledge. Our emotions often have physical effects on our bodies and correspondingly, our bodies have effects on our emotions. When you are in the most distress, sometimes the most useful thing you can do is to directly deal with what your body needs. Remember the acronym TIPP, which stands for Temperature, Intense Exercise, Paced Breathing, and Paired muscle relaxation.

Temperature refers to lowering your body temperature. When we are emotionally overwhelmed, frequently we feel hot. Doing something to cool down, literally, can help you figuratively cool down. Options include taking a cool shower, splashing your face with cold water, holding an ice cube, or even just turning up the AC. Using the physical cold can help gain a little bit of emotional stability.

Intense exercise can also help deal with intense emotional distress. Anything that pushes your body can be helpful, even if you aren't in great shape or prone to regularly exercising. You don't have to run a marathon. Just sprinting down the street, a couple times or doing jumping jacks until you are tired can help. Exercise increases oxygen levels and oxygen flow, which does a lot of good work to decrease stress levels. It also releases good endorphins which can make you feel better. And, if you are prone to unhealthy behavior when you are feeling this upset, it is harder to do it when you are totally exhausted.

Paced Breathing is the third strategy. It seems so simple but controlling your breath can have a profound impact on your mental state. Managing your breath can calm you down and make you feel much more relaxed. There are many types of breathing exercises. It could be as simple as just taking several deep breaths, trying to totally fill your lungs with air. If you would prefer a more formal exercise, try a technique called "box breathing." With this technique, you inhale for a count of four, hold your breath for a count of four, and then exhale for a count of four, and then hold four. There are four sets of four, one on each stage: inhale, holding it, exhale, holding it. Focus on this steady breathing until you feel better.

The last part of the acronym is Paired Muscle Relaxation. Research has shown that muscles relax more after being purposefully tightened than if you just try to relax them directly. In this exercise, first you purposefully tighten a muscle and then relax it and allow it to rest. This will be more relaxing than just directly trying to relax. Try this technique by focusing on groups of muscles such as your arms or back. Consciously put as much tension into the muscle as you can for five full seconds and then relax. Let go of the tightness. This will help you begin to relax as well.

Hopefully these four skills can help you start to cope with whatever is being so emotionally distressing.

None of them are solving the problem, but when you are overwhelmingly upset it is impossible to think clearly.

Distracting Yourself: ACCEPTS

Sometimes it is important to distract yourself even when you aren't in crisis. Maybe you are waiting for a particularly difficult conversation to start or you have an interview in the morning that you are already prepared for but is making you anxious. In these situations, remember the acronym ACCEPTS. ACCEPTS stands for Activities, Contribution, Comparison, Emotion, Push away, Thoughts, and Sensations. Like the previous skill, this will not solve the problem, but it will give you the chance to keep your emotions in check until you are in a position to directly address the cause of the emotions.

The first suggestion is "Activities" and this can be just about anything healthy. As long as it won't hurt you in either the long term or the short term, it can be a great activity to distract yourself. Play a game that you love, watch a show, read a book. You could even make apple sauce or go for a walk. Do the dishes! Sometimes, you can end up having a very productive day just trying to avoid thinking about what is bothering you. Be careful, though. Do not let this be an excuse to do something harmful or that you have general problems with. If you have trouble with money, your activity should not be shopping. If you struggle with over-eating, do not eat to distract yourself. The goal is to replace our existing unhealthy coping behaviors with healthy behaviors that cause no harm.

The second part of the acronym is Contribution. This asks you to do something nice for someone else. Doing something kind or beneficial to another person can be very helpful in relieving emotional distress. At the very least, the act of doing something nice will help get your mind off of your problems. But even more than that, doing good for other people helps us feel good about ourselves. It leads to a sense of being valuable and important in the world, because you are a person capable of helping others. This does not have to be something big. Try cooking dinner for someone else, mowing the neighbor's lawn, or volunteering at a cause you love. Find a way to give to someone else and you will feel better in your own skin.

If doing physical activities isn't working as well as you would hope, you can try to deal with emotions with mental techniques as well. One of those techniques is Comparison. This technique asks you to put your life in perspective. Have you faced more difficult challenges than whatever is bothering you at this moment? It is possible that it is in fact the most intense emotion you've ever experienced, which might mean you should jump up to the TIPP section. But very likely, it is not. It may feel, at first, just as bad as you ever felt, but when you think about it, you have overcome worst. And even if it is the worst you've ever experienced, other people have suffered more than you. If you are at home safe, someone is without a home. If you do not have a home, at least you aren't struggling to find safety from a national disaster. The goal is not to make you feel guilty or to add more pain to what you are currently experiencing. The goal is to remind yourself that what you are going through is survivable. You have survived it in the past, and if you haven't, other people have. It is possible to get through the emotions you are experiencing.

Emotions is the next part of distraction. This strategy involves consciously trying to evoke the opposite emotion of what you are feeling. If you are feeling anxious, try meditating or doing some of the breathing and paired muscle relaxation above. If you are sad, try googling pictures of adorable animals. If you want to laugh, watch a comedian you love. Sometimes adding the opposite emotion to the situation can help temper your current negative emotions.

Push away is the next part of tolerating distress. This is simply the project of not thinking about the distressing thing. Every time it comes to your mind, consciously push it away, don't let yourself dwell on it. Distract yourself with other activities or thoughts. Sometimes this is difficult to do on its own, so it often combines with the next part of the acronym, Thoughts. Thoughts refers to replacing negative, anxious thoughts with things that busy your mind. These are often very simple and straightforward. Say the alphabet backwards, count to the highest number you can, do a cross-word puzzle. Read poetry out loud. Do anything that fills your mind and keeps it away from the thing that is bothering you so much.

The last part of the acronym is Sensation. This refers to using your five senses to self-soothe during times of distress. You could watch a YouTube video of a walk in the forest or if you can, go on that walk yourself. You could take a warm bath or shower and enjoy the smells of your bath products. You could stroke your pet and feel their soft fur. Anything that fills your senses and is enjoyable can be a way to self-soothe through sensation. Just laying in a comfortable bed and enjoying the way the blankets feel can help, if you let yourself enjoy it.

Deal without Having Control – IMPROVE

The previous skills presumed that there was a space of time between the present and when you will be able to deal with the problem. The goal is to distract yourself until you can solve it. Unfortunately, we cannot solve all of the problems that we are in. The circumstances can be small or large, but we will all face times where we don't have control over something unpleasant. In these cases, it isn't possible to just distract yourself until you can fix it. Instead, you have to think about distress tolerance in a different way.

There is yet another acronym for dealing with this type of situation: IMPROVE. IMPROVE stands for Imagery, Meaning, Prayer, Relaxation, One Thing in the moment, Vacation, and Encouragement.

Imagery involves imagining the problem being solved and everything turning out okay. You may not have much ability to affect the outcome of the problem, but there is no point in focusing on all the ways it can go wrong as opposed to thinking about ways that you could end up being okay. If you don't have control, the only choice you have is about how to think about the situation. Obsessing over negative outcomes won't change the outcome, but it will make you feel worse. In that sort of case, try to focus on things turning out okay.

Meaning is about looking for meaning even in the toughest situations. What will you learn from even this? A painful event can help you be more empathetic to others. Maybe you'll have to meet new people. Maybe this will be a turning point in your life and you'll be able to do something different. Find a purpose and a reason to give to your present moment and it will be much easier to tolerate. Human beings are creatures driven by meaning. Athletes push themselves through pain to get stronger all the time and they even enjoy it. If you can figure out how the current circumstance will make you stronger or wiser, it will be much easier to bear.

Prayer can take many different forms. If there is a particular religious tradition that means something to you, pray in the way that resonates. If you do not have a religious tradition, you can pray to the universe or to a generic higher power. The goal is to surrender your problems to something higher than yourself and acknowledge that your earthly control has no ability to solve what you are dealing with.

Relaxation is important, even in the more long-term type of distress tolerance we are talking about now. We tend to tense up in stressful situations and it can make things even more unpleasant. Calm yourself down, whether it be through breathing, a hot bath, or a relaxing walk. However, you best self-soothe, make sure to use it whenever you feel yourself getting tenser.

One thing in the moment is asking you to use mindfulness skills. We will talk about mindfulness in more detail later in the book, but the goal is to stay in the present. Avoid thinking about old issues or possible future issues. Neither of them will be able to help you in solving the present situation. Find a single thing to focus on and keep your focus there. It could be painting a wall, your breath, or even your homework. Keeping your mind focused on one thing can make your emotions feel less overwhelming.

For the next part of the acronym, Vacation, ideally, you'd be able to get away from it all. You could leave your home and take a break from all the stressors. Most of us aren't able to do this, especially not during a moment of crisis. Instead, take a vacation in your mind. Imagine yourself somewhere beautiful and peaceful. Stroll around a lake at sunset or see the tropical rainforest birds. Stay in this place in your mind as long as you want to and maybe you will be able to return to the present better able to tolerate your circumstances.

The last part of the acronym is Encouragement. Many of us habitually seek encouragement from external sources, but it does not have to be from someone else to be effective. Repeat encouraging phrases to yourself. Tell yourself you can get through this and that you can improve this moment. You can motivate yourself and get through this challenging time.

Chapter 8: Behavioral Activation or, just do it!

When people are feeling depressed, it is common for there to be what is called "anhedonia" or loss of pleasure and interest in previously enjoyed activities. Decreasing interest in what you usually do is not just a symptom of depression but can happen with any low mood or anxiety. With stress and PTSD, there can be a general sense of having low responsiveness to rewards and activities. Basically, many mental health conditions manifest by an individual just not doing much of anything.

Behavioral activation targets that phenomenon directly. Research shows that it is as effective as cognitive therapy in combatting depression (Cuijpers et al., 2007). Behavioral activation is in many ways easier than many of the cognitive strategies that we've talked about already. You don't have to have a nuanced sense of your own mind in order to do behavioral activation.

The basic idea of behavioral activation is that depression and low mood often occurs when individual behavior is responded to with negative reinforcement. A person tries to do something, and it leads to a punishment or negative outcome. When that starts to happen, the individual does less and less, in an effort to avoid negative reinforcement. This is an understanding of depression which is more about the environment around the person and less about their inner life or cognitive features.

In line with this, behavior activation tries to decrease depression by increasing activities, counteracting avoidance behaviors, and increasing the experience of pleasurable things and positive reinforcement. The goal is to find more pleasant things to do and to actually do them. Instead of dwelling in your own mind to solve your problems, you change what you do on a daily basis and see what happens.

The first step in behavioral activation is to have a good sense of how you act in different situations. What are the activities you do on a daily basis at work? At home? What do you do when you are confronted with something unpleasant? What do you do for fun? Identify patterns of behavior and try to keep an eye out for cases of negative reinforcement. Are there things in your life that you do that make you feel worse? It can be helpful to keep a detailed record of your behavior and moods. Maybe write down what you are doing every half-hour and how you feel. In doing this you may discover that you don't have the same level of depression all day every day. You may also find that there are things you do in order to feel better that don't work or actually make you feel worse. For instance, if you drink to feel better, close analysis may reveal that it doesn't actually work and leads to you feeling worse later.

Once you have a sense of your current behavior, the next goal is to start to think about changing it. The goal in behavioral activation is to change the behavior and to use the behavior change to adjust your mind.

Ask yourself the question, are there things you would be doing if you weren't depressed? If you think about times when you aren't depressed, are there things you do that you enjoy? Try to experiment with positive activities.

One activity you can do is brainstorm twenty activities that you enjoy and that are healthy. This means that they should be things that are consistent with the life you want to live and not things that you have reason to think will make you feel worse in the medium or long term. Examples might be reading a book, going to a movie, playing video games, walking the dog. It could be anything that gives you pleasure. Make a list, physically. Actually, write it down.

Once you have the list of twenty things that give you pleasure, go through and rate the pleasure or benefit you get out of the activity from 1-10. Maybe you really enjoy movies, so they would be a 7. Maybe walking the dog is fun but not amazing, so it would be a 3. Maybe going to concerts is one of your favorite things, so that would be a 9. This doesn't have to be exact. Go with your gut about the various rankings.

Once you have ranked the amount of pleasure you get out of each activity, then go through again and rank them on the basis of their accessibility, with 1 being easily accessible and 10 being more difficult. Going to a movie is pretty easy, so that gets a 3. Concerts are more expensive and rarer, so that gets an 8. Walking the dog is really easy, so it gets a 1.

Then, after you have assigned all twenty activities both numbers subtract the accessibility number from the pleasure number. This will tell you the activities that you find a combination of accessible and pleasurable. It will essentially give you a clue on something that is relatively easy to do and gives a lot back for the ease.

Then, once you have an idea of activities, just do one of them. You may not feel like you are in the mood and it may feel inauthentic to do it. Before you get started, you may not even feel like you would have any fun. Try to do it anyway. Sometimes our minds lie to us and things feel very difficult to begin with. The only way you will be able to know how you feel when you do these things is to actually try and do them. When you do one of these activities, pay careful attention of your mood. How do you feel when you've done the pleasurable activity?

Most of the time, you will find that you feel better. It is easy to forget how good simple things feel in the face of larger emotional pain. Just the small thing of going to a movie or going for a walk can feel nice and pleasurable. It's important not to expect this small step to change your life all by itself. You won't be cured because you went to a movie. That is too much of an expectation for the simple activity. On the other hand, take seriously it just being a nice time. Something doesn't have to be enormous in order to be impactful. One of the things that depression does is cause us to forget how to have a simple, nice time.

This experimentation with new behavior should be continuous and ongoing. If you find that the activity you selected is harder than you thought, take that into account. If you get less pleasure out of it than you thought, factor that in. Try to do different activities and experiment about how they make you feel. The goal is to make step by step changes that help bring you to a happier place.

This is especially beneficial if you can replace old activities that made you unhappy with new ones that make you happier. Perhaps you spent four hours at night watching the news while sipping wine. If you look at your activity log, you can see that you typically feel depressed and unhappy. And, even more, the wine makes the next morning more difficult. This would be a good example of an activity to replace. Maybe one day, instead of watching the news during that time, you invite a friend out for a movie. Trying something different may break up the depressed mood which is typical during that time. Compare how the movie makes your mood feel to how the news and wine routine used to make you feel.

In general, one of the things that behavioral activation teaches is that avoidance behaviors don't typically work. Maybe the reason that you stay inside and don't reach out to friends is because you find it difficult to reach out. If that is stressful, often we have behaviors which avoid the stressful event. On the other hand, that avoidance strategy doesn't help the overall problem get any better. It makes it harder to address difficult issues and makes the long-term more difficult, even if it feels okay in the short term.

It is useful to analyze what your avoidance patterns are. What behaviors do you do in an attempt to avoid painful emotions or events? Maybe you sleep too much in order to avoid demands being made on you when you are awake. Thinking about your problems obsessively, known as rumination, can counter-intuitively be an avoidance strategy. By just thinking about your problems, you are not doing anything to fix them or help your life. A big problem with this type of avoidance strategy is that it can have a very negative effect on mood.

One way to think about avoidance behaviors is with the acronym ACTION. ACTION stands for Assess behavior and mood, choose alternative behaviors, Try the alternate behaviors, integrate alternative behaviors into a routine, Observe the outcome of behavior, and Never give up.

Assessing the behavior and mood is asking you to analyze your current behavior. Are you doing something to avoid negative feelings? What is your current mood? How does your current behavior help or hurt your life as a whole?

After you have assessed the current behavior, then you Choose an alternative behavior. Like we discussed before, there are things in your life that you enjoy, many of which you've stopped doing because you don't feel good. If you actively choose to replace an avoidant behavior with an alternative, healthy behavior you can improve your mood.

After you've chosen the behavior, you have to Try that behavior. Is this new behavior helping your mood? Does it effectively fill the space that the avoidant behavior used to fill?

Then, Integrate this behavior into a regular routine. Instead of the behaviors which you typically do that lower your mood, you should try to have the mood-elevating behaviors take over the space in your life. Establish a routine based around behaviors that make you feel good, even if it is only momentarily.

Observe the outcome of the behaviors. How do the new behaviors make you feel? What new things do they add to your life? Have they improved the situation in a larger way?

And last, never give up. Trying a new behavior only once is unlikely to lead to any significant change. Overcoming depression and bad moods takes a lot of hard work and there will not be easy, instant answers. Sometimes there will be setbacks, but instead of giving up, you should remain committed to the overall goal.

When you are making changes, it is often a better idea to make a change one step at a time instead of all at once. Sometimes we wake up and feel like we are totally going to change our lives. That rarely sticks. Instead of doing that, pick one specific negative behavior to change and focus your energy on changing that.

Works Cited

Cuijpers, P., Van Straten, A., & Warmerdam, L. (2007). Behavioral activation treatments of depression: a meta-analysis. *Clinical psychology review, 27*(3), 318-326.

Chapter 9: Problem Solving Skills

Problem solving skills are universal because all people encounter problems, and anyone can benefit from having a step by step approach to solving them. Problem solving involves, importantly, the attitude that problems can be solved or at least improved. There are four distinct steps.

1) Identify the problem and set goals. These goals should be realistic.
2) Come up with possible solutions. This is often called brainstorming.
3) Evaluate the possible solutions and then decide which one is worth trying.
4) Try the possible solution. After you try it, evaluate the consequences and decide if it in fact solved the problem.

Good problem solving allows you to deal with many things in life. It leads to better coping skills, which leads to an improved life and a better moon. Often, bad problem-solving skills can become a vicious cycle. If you have a problem and you fail to solve it, it can lead to a variety of other problems. There can be a negative cycle where things get worse and worse.

Focusing on solving problems can be empowering. When you solve problems, you feel more in control of your life and that can make everything easier. Good problem-solving skills are associated with better emotional adjustment and when you have poor problem-solving skills, you will experience more distress. Poor problem-solving skills are associated with drug and alcohol addiction, criminal behavior, and generalized distress.

Problem solving skills can be learned! People can get better at problem solving and you can, too.

The most important thing is to develop a positive problem orientation. Positive problem orientations are when you view problems as a challenge where it is possible to improve. It means you believe that you have the ability to solve problems. It also means you believe that successful problem solving can include instances of failure and you understand that this is part of the process of solving a problem.

In contrast, negative problem orientation views problems as unsolvable and frightening. These people view situations as impossible to improve and they do not think they themselves have the ability to solve problems. When they run into initial failure, they think that means the problem cannot be solved.

When you have a positive problem orientation, you see difficulties as normal life challenges. You try to find solutions. This optimism is a choice that you need to make about your life. Try to act optimistic and look for new possibilities. When you start to find new solutions to your problems, you will find that you naturally start to be more optimistic. You will learn that it is possible to make things better and that commitment will help you make so many things better.

After you have made a commitment that solving problems is possible, the first step is to identify what problems you have. It is very important to be able to determine what your problems are and set realistic goals. Problems can be one-time events or ongoing and repeated. When you have a negative problem orientation, it is common to avoid facing your problem. This makes it even more important to face it.

It is best to define your problem as specifically as possible. Having the problem be "I cannot communicate well with my wife" is less good than saying "when my wife disagrees with me, I find it hard to contain my anger." Being clear and specific makes it much more approachable to think of solutions.

Here are some questions that can help you define your problem:

- What happened or did not happen that bothers you?
- Who is involved? Where does the problem happen? When does the problem happen?
- Why is this problem difficult for you?
- What do you do to avoid the problem currently?
- What do you hope will happen?

These questions will help you determine what the problem is and what your goals should be. When you set goals, you should have those goals be SMART. This stands for specific, measurable, achievable, relevant, time-bound. Specific goals are focused. They are defined by exactly what outcome you want to have happen. They are not vague. The problem with vague goals is that is very difficult to know what exactly what you want and it will be much more difficult to determine what you should do to meet them.

They should be measurable, which is part of having them be specific. You should be able to determine in an objective way when and if you met your goal. This helps your mind to not pay tricks on you. It prevents you from moving your own goalposts.

Goals should also be achievable. You should set targets that are possible to reach. That is the only way you learn that you are effective and capable of solving problems. If you set yourself up to fail, it will just be frustrating. You will find yourself discouraged. Making your goals possible to meet is much more productive.

Relevant goals are those that are consistent with your other goals and your overall life course. This helps the goal be more important to you and makes it more likely that you work to solve it.

Time-bound is the last feature goals should have. This means you should set at least a provisional time frame when you are going to achieve your goal. Having no time-frame means that you can continually put things off and push them away. Giving yourself a deadline encourages you to get started.

Once you have a clear sense of the problem and a SMART goal, the next step is to brainstorm solutions. Finding solutions to these problems may be difficult. If you knew a better way to manage your life, you probably would already be doing it. Problem-solving involves forcing yourself to step outside your comfort zone and think beyond the mindset you are used to. In order to do that, the idea is to brainstorm. Generate as many solutions as possible and with as much variety. Push yourself to come up with as many things you can think of, even if some of them seem far-fetched or seemingly impossible. Defer judgment on whether or not they are good solutions. The first step is simply to think of them.

Ask yourself questions like these to help yourself come to new solutions:

- What would you tell someone else that had this problem?
- What would a loved one suggest you do to solve this problem?
- What things have you done to handle similar situations in the past?
- How do you overcome problems in other parts of your life?
- What are some positive elements of the situation that can help you solve this problem?
- Is there anything about the problem that cannot be changed?

These questions can help push yourself to come up with new possibilities. As you brainstorm, write down the list of solutions so you can look at them all at once.

Once you have a list of solutions, the next step is to evaluate them. It can be very empowering to look at all the possibilities in front of you and consider which one is the most beneficial. You want to evaluate the likelihood that the solutions with solve the actual problem and meet your realistic goals. You also want to consider any other effects that the problem may have. Ask yourself what the short term and long term benefits and drawbacks of each solution are? What are some good things and bad things that might happen if you engage in this solution? Some questions you might ask yourself include:

- How will this solution affect me?
- How will this solution affect other people?
- How will I feel after implementing this solution?
- Is this solution consistent with what I value?
- How plausible does this solution feel?
- How much time and effort will this solution require?

These questions can help you determine which solutions are viable.

Once you have selected a solution, the next step ist o make a plan. You need to actually implement the solution. The plan should be as specific and concrete as you can make it. Try writing out what you will do, day by day, being specific as to the time and place. When you are planning things, make sure to prepare for the worst-case scenario. Sometimes when you engage in solutions that involve going to other people like your boss or spouse, they may not respond in the way that you would like them to. Be realistic about the negative possibilities and only go through with it if it seems worth the risk.

In order to practice engaging in the solution, use your imagination to visualize and rehearse the plan. Imagine doing the solution in your mind. Close your eyes and visualize doing what you need to do, focusing on what you would see, feel, hear, and experience. Use this process to project forward any obstacles that you could confront.

After you have planned and rehearsed the solution, the next step is to actually try it out. Think of this as an experiment which will provide additional data. It is critical not to get discouraged prematurely. Things don't always work out on the first attempt and it is important not to have the mindset that things are either perfect right away or a total failure. You may continue to problem solve, but that is normal. Life is just a series of problem-solving opportunities.

While you are engaging in this process, it is useful to develop thoughts that help you cope. Come up with optimistic or positive things that you can come back to as ways to reassure yourself that you are doing the right thing. What would you say to yourself ot help you cope with this situation? What advice would you give to a friend who was dealing with this situation? If you were feeling optimistic about this situation, what would you think?

If the initial attempt to solve the problem doesn't work, go back to brainstorming. You will be able to solve the problem, or at least improve it, as long as you keep trying.

Chapter 10: Mindfulness

Mindfulness is an important part of learning to be emotionally and mentally healthy. Mindfulness skills help you learn to be in the present moment in a nonjudgmental way and to refrain from acting impulsively. Modern mindfulness is based on ancient Buddhist principles, but they have been scientifically validated again and again. Learning mindfulness helps you learn techniques for focusing your thoughts and attention on the present. You will develop increased control of your mind and you will learn the skill of observation and attention.

Most other skills in this book require the ability to step back from your experience and evaluate them without judgment. Mindfulness is one way to learn that skill. Mindfulness involves being attentive to the present moment and the task at hand without being distracted by intervening thoughts.

Mindfulness is about increasing awareness of the moment you are in. This means you have to practice bringing your attention to the present moment and training your mind to only focus on one thing at time. It Is often useful to practice paying attention to only one thing at a time and learning to gently draw your attention back to the thing you are supposed to be paying attention to when your mind inevitably wanders. Learning how to pay attention to one thing at a time is sometimes called "one-mindedness."

As you practice mindfulness skills, remember that your attention wandering is part of the point. The goal is to learn how to bring your attention back to the present moment and what you want to focus on. In order to learn how to do that, your mind will have to wander. Forgive yourself for this inevitable wandering—that is how you will learn to get better.

Practicing mindfulness is like doing repetitions at the gym. With repetition, the mind learns the skills necessary to keep attention and develops the strength to be able to bring attention back to the present. Even just noticing when your mind wanders helps you develop the skills necessary.

You can practice mindfulness in any activity. When you are eating, for instance, put down your phone and turn off the TV. Keep your attention entirely on the food. Take time to activate your senses. Smell the food, look at the food. Notice things about the food that you've never seen before. When you take a bite, close your eyes and focus your entire attention on the sensation in your mouth. What does it taste like? What does it feel like? How does it feel against your tongue? Learning to keep your attention on one thing like that can help you learn to experience the world in a new way.

There are four steps to being mindful and practicing mindfulness.

1) **Choose an activity**. This can really be any activity. When you get skilled at mindfulness, you can strive to bring it into any part of your life. But as you are getting started, it is helpful to have a specific activity that you

intend to do mindfully. Examples include spending time with your children and pets, playing a sport, engaging in a hobby like knitting or sewing. Even just going for a walk-through nature can be engaged in mindfully.

2) **Focus on the activity**. Once you are engaged in the activity, focus on it. Be in the present on the activity. Keep your mind and senses engaged in what you are doing. Don't check your phone, don't think about other things. Keep your focus where you intend to keep it.

3) **Notice when your attention wanders**. It is natural for your attention to wander. That is part of the process of mindfulness. Our brains are busy generating countless thoughts. The important part is to notice when our attention is distracted from what we are intending to focus on. It is a skill in itself to just be aware of the distraction.

4) **Gently bring your attention back**. The last step, after accepting that your attention has wandered, is to bring your attention back to the present moment. Do this kindly and without judgment. The goal is to move yourself softly back to where you want your attention to be.

It is important to be patient with yourself. Most of us have had experience with puppies at some point in our life. When you first start to train a puppy to stay, it doesn't work very well. You turn around and the puppy follows you immediately. When this happens, you don't get mad at the puppy. It is just a puppy! She needs to be trained. That's the way your mind is. Your mind has not been trained to be mindful yet. The process of training it is how you will learn to keep your attention on what you want it to be on.

If it would be helpful for you to have an activity dedicated to practicing mindfulness, a good one is to count your breaths. Sit quietly and count each breath – saying one as you draw a deep breath in and two as you slowly breath out. Three on the inhalation, four on the exhalation, and so on. Count up to ten and then start over at one. When you find yourself getting distracted, gently move your attention back to the breath. It is helpful to set a timer for ten or twenty minutes and try to focus for the whole time. Try establishing a time in your day to do this every day and you will improve very quickly.

One feature of a mindful stance is that it is not judgmental. As you increase awareness of the present moment, it is important to avoid passing judgment on your experience. When you are mindful, you experience the world as it actually is, not as it should be. We make all sorts of judgments about the world, typically deciding how we should think and feel in advance. When we meet someone new, we extrapolate from their clothes and hair. When we order a dish at a restaurant, we look at it and think that we know how it is going to taste.

Often, we experience the world as we think it "should" be as opposed to how it is. When you are trying to be mindful, observe yourself making judgments. Watch the way that you make conclusions about your experiences before they even happen. As much as possible, resist this urge and return your attention to the world in front of you. Mindfulness helps you learn to describe your experience without judgment, therefore helping you separate your thoughts from the actual situation at hand.

Try looking at a piece of art and observing it without making judgments about it. Do not think about whether or not it is ugly or beautiful, cheap or expensive. Instead, focus on the colors and shapes. Try to pick out marks made by a brush or pen. Spend time just looking at it, as if you had never seen a painting before.

Avoiding positive judgment is just as important as resisting negative judgment, because positive judgments are reflecting attachment to things being a particular way. If you have positive judgment toward parts of the world, then you will experience distress if that world changes.

One way of thinking of this stance of non-judgment is known as "beginner's mind." This is the idea that you should interact with the world as if you have never experienced before, like a child. If you try to avoid judgment and baggage, you can experience things in a fresh and interesting way. Beginner's mind is dropping our preconceived notions about something and interacting it without expectation. This leads to better experiences, where you can interact with the object as it truly is, without being clouded by prejudgments.

It is particularly helpful when interacting with people. Beginner's mind leads to better relationships because it allows you to treat each interaction with a person like a new beginning. You won't judge them on whether or not they are meeting the ideal that you have for them and you won't let your experience be colored by past negative experiences. Maybe someone was mean to you once. Normally, this would shape every future interaction with that person. But perhaps they were just having a bad day or if it is nothing permanent. Instead of holding on to the memory of the previous bad interaction, you can let it go and experience each moment with this person anew.

It can also lead to less anxiety. Normally, the feeling of anxiety happens because we are making predictions about negative possibilities. We think that something bad will happen because we think that this is the sort of thing where bad things happen. Adopting beginner's mind means opening yourself up to gentle curiosity, letting go of your existing ideas about what the possibilities are and what is scary about them. The goal is to embrace not knowing what is going to happen, to embrace being in the moment and finding thankfulness in the present for what you are doing and who you are interacting with.

In many ways, mindfulness is about learning how to be effective. When you increase awareness on the present moment, you will learn how to keep your eyes on your goals and not be distracted by unnecessary things. Sometimes people are so focused on being right or winning arguments that they do not keep in mind what they actually want in any given scenario. For instance, if you get in an argument with a cab driver over the air conditioning, think to yourself if it is worth getting angry and possibly leading to him refusing to take you to your destination. Maybe it is better to just subside and let the situation past.

Being right is not the same thing as being skillful. Being effective is about learning how to focus on being skillful, not being right. The idea is to learn how to choose your battles and experience the world in a more peaceful and gentle way.

Judgments are often the result of negative emotions. If a situation happens and you feel strongly about it, you'll often judge it as bad. However, the problem is that the judgment often triggers additional emotions. If something negative happens at work and it hurts you, leading you to judge the situation as "unfair," that might lead to additional pain. If you make a mistake, you have negative emotions from making the mistake. Then, you might judge yourself as stupid or inadequate, leading to additional pain.

Try to get in the habit of tracking when you are making judgments that escalate your emotions. Try using this worksheet or something in a similar format. I've filled out an example, so you can see how it works.

Situation	Emotions about the Situation	Judgments that resulted from the emotions	Extra Emotions triggered by the judgments	Outcome
I was driving and got stuck behind a tractor going very slowly	Frustrated	What an idiot for driving on the main road. This is unfair that it is happening to me	Anger	I honked and got angrier. It put me in a terrible mood when I got into work.

When you are practicing mindfulness, get in the habit of "noting" when you have particular thoughts or feelings pass your mind. Imagine your thoughts like soap bubbles, floating through a clear sky. When you notice them, gently touch them with a label and let them pop. When you feel a wave of sadness, note that you are sad and let it go. If you feel worry, note that you felt worry, and let it go. This can be helpful in avoiding judgments particularly – if you experience a judgment, note that you have done so and let it go.

Chapter 11: Radical Acceptance

So far, we have talked about many skills for handling intense emotions, from cognitive skills about changing your thoughts to more behavior oriented ones. We have talked about mindfulness and emotional regulation. The most important skill, however, is radical acceptance. Radical acceptance is the idea that even in the most painful situation, we have to accept it. This is what makes it radical.

Acceptance does not mean approval. Acceptance means acknowledging that the situation you are in is reality and there is nothing you can do about it. Many of us spend a lot of time refusing to accept the reality of a situation. We think, this isn't fair or why is this happening to me. These things just increase our suffering. Pain is unavoidable in life, but suffering isn't. Pain is what happens when something bad happens, suffering is what happens when we fight against it and refuse to accept it.

Acceptance is non-judgmental. Accepting something doesn't mean you are saying it is good or bad, it simply means that you are acknowledging reality as it is. Imagine that you are driving to work, and you are stuck in traffic. This is unpleasant, in many ways. You might get in trouble for being late to work. But if you think "this is unfair" and "I can't believe this is happening," then you are just going to increase how upset you are. Honking and tailgating the car in front of you won't get you to work any faster. It just increases unhappy you are. Imagine the difference between being upset and worked up the whole slow commute to work and simply accepting that you are going to be late and being at peace with the car.

Accepting reality is the necessary shift that helps genuine and permanent change. You cannot change anything unless you have first accepted it. If you are constantly fighting reality, you'll be spending all your time and energy pretending the problem doesn't exist as opposed to trying to fix the problem. Acceptance isn't about forgiveness or about letting anybody off the hook. The only goal is to put your own mind at ease and make yourself happier. You accept reality for yourself.

This is a difficult skill, but perhaps the most important one in the book. The more painful and difficult a situation is, the more difficult it will be to accept, and it will usually take longer. This is not a skill that can be mastered in one day, even at the best of times. To return to our driving example, if the conclusion of being late will inevitably getting fired, it will be much harder to accept than if it is simply a talking to for your boss. And, sometimes, you can get to the point of acceptance on something and then an additional event will trigger you to start reality again. Imagine Karen, a woman whose husband had an affair many years ago. She might have accepted it and moved on with their marriage, allowing things to improve tremendously. But then a young woman who looks like the person who Karen's husband had the affair with moves next door and Karen starts feeling angry and upset once again. She might have to go back to accepting the reality and not fighting against it.
As you are working on accepting reality, it might get frustrating. But even if you can accept the painful

reality for only thirty seconds, that is thirty seconds less suffering than you would have otherwise. Gradually those thirty seconds will grow and grow until you are able to sustain it.

Most of us have had painful situations in our life that we have naturally come to accept. Perhaps a loved one died or you did not receive a job that you were hoping for. It hurts, but eventually it is possible to come to terms and accept the new reality. There is a difference between fighting a situation and coming to terms with it. Most of the time, you feel lighter and more at ease once you've accepted a situation. The situation has less power over you and the pain diminishes. When you think about it, there is less emotional pain.

How do you practice accepting reality?

The first and most important part is that you make the choice to accept it. You have to buy into the idea that accepting reality will be helpful and make you feel better. If you don't buy in, then there's nothing to be done. Part of this involves directly facing what is happening. Before you can accept something, you have to develop the self-awareness to face it and look at it directly.

Second, if you decide to work on acceptance, the next step is to make a commitment to yourself to accept the reality that you are fighting. You need to make yourself a promise that starting now, you are going to accept the situation. The promise is not going to solve it by itself—typically even after you have made a commitment you will find yourself going back to fighting reality, making judgments, thinking about unfair the situation is and so on.

Third, you must learn to notice when you start fighting reality again. Notice when you start thinking the situation is not fair or wishing that life was otherwise.

Fourth, turn your mind back to acceptance. Every time you notice yourself fighting reality and insisting that reality isn't fair, remind yourself you made yourself a promise to accept reality. Remind yourself of your commitment and turn your mind back toward acceptance. You will need to do this over and over again in order to get the hang of out.

One thing to acknowledge is that everything has a cause. Even this thing that is causing you pain had to have happened, because the way the world went. If you think about it, a tsunami is a tragedy that hurts a lot of people, but the reason why it happened is the laws of physics. It had to have happened that way, because it was caused in a particular way. There is no way for it to have been otherwise, given the way the world was.

It is sometimes useful to think of the whole universe as a series of causes. Everything is causing other things, knocking around like balls on a pool table. Any individual thing had to have happened the way it did, given all the other factors and all the things that went into causing it. There is an inevitability to the past and the future. There was no other way that it could have gone.

People tend to have some difficulties with this skill. One thing that people think is that accepting reality means giving up. But that is not the case. Acceptance just means giving up fighting the reality of the situation, it does not preclude you trying to solve the problem. It means that you no longer waste time and energy thinking that a situation isn't fair or undeserved. You instead focus on what is necessary to fix the situation.

Second, sometimes people confuse acceptance of the moment for accepting things that haven't happened yet. When they try to accept the end of a relationship, they think that what they need to accept is a lifetime of loneliness. The thing to remember is accepting reality, not things that haven't happened yet. You need to learn to accept that your previous relationship is ended, but there is no reason to accept that there won't be a relationship in the future. We cannot possibly know what the future will hold. It is hard enough accepting the present and the past, there is no reason to make things more difficult by trying to accept the future.

When you are struggling with being alone, what you need to accept is not having a partner at the present moment. There is no need of trying to accept that you will be alone for the rest of your life. The goal is to try to keep your mind in the present and to practice mindfulness. Radical acceptance cannot help with concerns that are future oriented.

Another thing that people might think is that acceptance means that they need to accept negative judgments about themselves. Someone might think, how can I accept that I am a bad person? Just as we cannot accept the future, we also cannot accept judgments. Judgments aren't facts, they are perceptions of reality. You have to accept the facts of your life, but the judgments are extraneous. So, for instance, if you think you are a bad person because you were addicted to drugs and lashed out to people who cared about you, you need to accept those realities. The reality of addiction and the reality of how you treated others are what you need to accept. Bundling that into a judgment of being a bad person is not what you need to accept and, indeed, is probably actively unhelpful.

A large problem with acceptance is the idea that the situation is just too awful and too painful to accept. It is easy to feel that something is so horrible that it is impossible to accept. If you've experienced abuse, you could feel that it is too awful to accept. One issue that happens here is the confusion of acceptance with forgiveness. You are practicing acceptance for yourself, not anyone else. You accept it because it will make your life easier, not because it forgives the person who hurts you. Acceptance doesn't work if you do it for other people and it isn't about other people.

Sometimes people think that we need to stay angry in order to protect ourselves. You might worry that accepting the situation will make you vulnerable. You feel like you are angry, withdrawing, and resentful as a way of protecting yourself from hurt. The problem is that the way that you are trying to protect yourself is causing you suffering in the present. You aren't actually preventing yourself from being hurt by being angry, but you are causing yourself emotional pain.

Additionally, remember that acceptance doesn't mean approval. Reality, in a sense, doesn't care about whether or not we approve of it. It exists, regardless of how we feel. The thing with acceptance is that is about acknowledging what reality is.

When you have started to accept things, you can then start to think about how you can make the best of things. This means many different things in different contexts. Sometimes it means that you should learn what you can from the situation and developed increased empathy from the experience. Sometimes you can think about ways you can make the situation better. It is important to think in the long term. Getting drunk may make you feel better in the moment, but it will not feel good in the morning. Try to meditate, read a good book, or take a walk-through nature.

One thing that may help is the realization that life isn't supposed to be easy. Life is supposed to be hard. Hard things happen to everybody. Hard things are part of what develops character and makes you the person who you are. When we think that life is unfair for having difficult things happening, we aren't acknowledging the reality that life is difficult.

There is always something you can learn from difficulty. You can always grow. Even if you feel wounded and damaged by whatever happened, it is possible for you to develop forward. Life never ends until it is over. Until that moment, there is always the possibility to get stronger and better as a human being. Accepting the reality of life is part of that.

Chapter 12: Improving Your Relationships with People

Social support is one of the most beneficial things you can have in your life, with positive effects on physical health, mental health, and your overall well-being. People with more social support are happier, healthier, and more productive. However, social support depends on your ability to display effective social behavior. For many people, ineffective social engagement is a large part of why they continue to have psychological difficulties.

Social skills are an important part of any attempt to recover from mental illness. Even if you think you have overall good social skills, it can never hurt to refine your ability to interact with other people and improve your interpersonal relationships. This can be particularly helpful if you struggle with social anxiety. A lot of social anxiety manifests as the sense of not knowing what to do or how to function. Learning specific social skills can make that easier.

"Interpersonal effectiveness" is the term that CBT practitioners use to measure the quality of social skills. It refers to a complicated interaction between several social skills and abilities that are necessary to achieve good social interaction, maintain relationships, and in general, obtain social goals in a variety of contexts. In general, interpersonal effectiveness means that you are able to attend to others and communicate effectively, plan behaviors, and demonstrate flexibility by adjusting your behavior to the feedback you get from others. In general, it means avoiding behaviors that others find unpleasant or difficult to deal with.

Our interpersonal behaviors are learned behaviors. We get our social skills predominately from early life, but they are reinforced by our social environment. Every time someone expresses approval or disapproval, a particular type of social skill is being reinforced.

This means that social skills and social success is largely cultural and context dependent. Within an individual culture, people are raised to understand the expectations that society has on them and the type of behavior which is positive. This does not always work smoothly, however. People can also develop either ineffective or dysfunctional social behaviors. Ineffective social behaviors do not tend to work particularly well, generally failing to produce positive outcomes. Dysfunctional interpersonal behaviors, on the other hand, often produce positive outcomes in the short term, despite being over all unpleasant. These are behaviors like a toddler throwing a tantrum. The toddler gets attention but is only excused for the behavior because of her age. If an adult threw a tantrum in a similar way, she might get immediate attention, but overall people would not want to interact with her.

Sometimes people run into problems when they move between social or cultural contexts and their social skills do not translate. Behavior which is effective in one context could be ineffective or damaging in another social context. Having the understanding to recognize when you have changed contexts is an important part of social skills.

How do you know whether or not you have positive social skills? In general, it is difficult to evaluate why you are having social problems yourself. If you know the behaviors which are causing you problems, then you can monitor yourself for instances of that behavior. Maybe you find yourself speaking without thinking and repeatedly insult people that way. If that is something you notice, you can keep track of when and how you do this behavior, in an effort to start the process of changing it.

If you have more systemic problems and you aren't sure directly why, then this might be a case where a couple sessions with a therapist would be useful. A therapist can do tactics like role plays and simulations to evaluate your social skills and help you determine where you are falling short. If there is someone in your life who you trust, you can ask them for their opinion. Try doing roleplays with them and test yourself in different types of social contexts to determine what behaviors you may be demonstrating that cause you social problems.

Here are some questions you can ask yourself to identify possible aspects of social behavior that you find difficult:

- What difficulties do you find yourself having in relationships?
- Do you have people that you are close to? Who? How often are you in contact with them? Can you be intimate with them?

- Are there times where you do not know what to do in social situations?
- Can you easily initiate and carry on a conversation with someone you do not know well?
- Do you get anxious in social contexts? What do you do when you get anxious in social situations?
- In times when you've felt challenged socially, what were the challenges? Did you have trouble expressing yourself? Controlling yourself?
- Do you have difficulty asking people to do something?
- Is it difficult for you to say no when you feel like you should?
- Have other people commented on things that you do socially in a negative way?
- Are there social situations that you avoid?
- Do you find it difficult to talk to certain types of people?
- How do you handle conflicts with others?
- When you ask people for something, what usually happens right afterward?
- Can you achieve your goals in social situations?
- When you have conflicts with others, how do they usually turn out?

Once you have a sense of what types of skills you struggle with, the goal then becomes to learn them. Skills are developed by a series of stages. First, you have to learn the skills and understand what you need to do. Then, you need to strengthen them through rehearsal and feedback. Finally, you need to generalize the skills and learn how to apply them in different contexts.

When you are learning social skills, it is important to place the focus on what is *effective* rather than what is "just right." It doesn't matter if you are doing something right if you aren't being effective. Letting go of the need to be right all the time is an important part of developing as a person, particularly in your social skills.

The next part of this chapter is going to go through several types of important social skills that you can incorporate into your repertoire.

Communication Skills

Communication is one of the most important things that we do with people, but it is also one of the most complicated. Communication involves many different things, including attention, fluency in speech, expressive ability, integrating multiple types of response, and non-verbal communication. In general, there are a variety of skills involved in the constructive sharing of thoughts and emotions.

In general, effective communication is about drawing people in as opposed to pushing people away. The goal is to establish the skill of increasing intimacy with people and learning to disclose parts of yourself to others in a way that invites them in. Specific parts of that include emotional disclosure ("I am really excited about this job interview that I'm going), demonstrations of understanding and support, ("I can see that you are upset. Would you like to talk about it?"), making positive requests ("I need someone to talk to. Can we talk?") and communicating positive feelings ("I really enjoyed our time together today.) Strengthening these aspects of communication is one of the most important ways to become more effective in social contexts.

Central to effectively communicating, also, is being able to smoothly transition between the roles of speaking and listening. Listening skills include the ability to pay attention when someone else is talking, acknowledging the speaker's comments with non-verbal behaviors like nodding and eye contact, and avoiding behaviors like interrupting or challenging views unnecessarily. Other listening skills involve: parroting (the ability to repeat back what the speaker said exactly), paraphrase (the ability to repeat back what is said in their own words to demonstrate understanding), reflection (being able to determine what the underlying emotion is underneath what is being expressed and asking the speaker if that is an accurate understanding) and validation.

Validation involves communicating to the speaker that their position is understood by conveying their own message back to them and affirming that the message is valid and agreed to by the listener. It is important to validate even if there is disagreement— you can validate that the speaker feels something and that you understand that they feel it, even if you do not fully agree with the content.

Speaking skills include the ability to accurately communicate what you are thinking or feeling. This means that speakers should be able to speak simply, clearly, and to the point. Complicated statements tend to be best understood when they are broken up into smaller and manageable parts, better allowing the listener to check in about their understanding with the speaker. Specific speaking skills include the ability to disclose the way that you are feeling about a situation and expressing affirmation or support of the other person.

A particularly important speaking skill is the ability to express negative emotions without any threats, demands, are put downs. The best way to express negative emotion is to link the emotion you are feeling in a matter-of-fact way with the behavior that caused it, keeping directly to the facts. Saying things like "I feel hurt when you make statements that make fun of me" is much more productive than saying "stop saying that, jerk."

Communication skills can be practiced every day and in every context. If it is too much to do all of them at once, pick one or two skills to focus on and practice. If attention is difficult for you, try to focus on paying close attention what people are saying and learning to adequately parrot their message back to them.

Conflict Management Skills

Conflicts are an inevitable part of life, but they can be very difficult to handle. People who are good at handling conflict are much better at dealing with interpersonal relationships on the whole.

One important thing in managing conflict is to learn to acknowledge the conflict in terms of the problem, rather than the person involved. It is also important to focus on "I" statements and speaking from your own perspective. The following pattern represents a general way to address and resolve conflicts.

- A statement of the issue with the conflict in a future oriented way. The goal is not to rehash the problem but to improve the situation moving forward. A good example of this would be to say, "I would like if we could sit down and talk about how we might address our disagreements more effectively in the future."
- A statement acknowledging the associated emotion in a personal way. The goal is not to make accusations about the other party. You should be focused on getting to an effective outcome, not exacting revenge on anyone else. Frame the effects of the situations in terms of the effects on you: "I am upset that this has become a problem."
- A goal statement that states what the ideal result would be. This should be a goal that is beneficial to both parties, eg "I hope we can resolve this to better maintain our friendship."
- A question that involves reaching out to the other person. This would be asking them how they are understanding this or dealing with the conflict.

A key part of any conflict resolution or addressing a conflict is the ability and willingness of everyone involved to listen to other people and not interrupt. Listening is a critical part of any resolution.

Effective problem solving can be improved by using the acronym SOLVES:

S= Specify the problem.
O = Outline your goals.
L= List the alternatives
V = View the likely consequences and select a promising alternative.
E = Establish and implement a plan
S = Survey the outcomes.

The first step is to specify the problem. The main element of this step is to clearly delineate what is the problem. What is the core of the issue? Ideally, this will involve both people in the relationship and take seriously what things both people are doing. Statements should consist of observable and identifiable facts. Try to avoid expressing blame or judgment about the other person.

The second step is to outline your goals. You should express what your personal goal is in the situation. The idea should be to specify what should be done to resolve the problem, not what the "right" thing to do would be. What do you want out of the problem? In this step it is important to be as specific as possible.

The third step is to list the alternatives. What are the possible routes to solving this problem? In this stage, brainstorming is encouraged. Many different things can be proposed. The idea is to create a list of possibilities.

The fourth step is to view the likely consequences and select a promising alternative. What do you project as the results of each of these alternatives? What do you think will happen if you try them? It is often a good idea to rank them in terms of the likelihood of achieving the objective and fulfilling the goals of the situation. The approach that is the most likely to solve the problem without creating new negative outcomes should be selected.

The fifth step is to establish the plan and implement it. Once the alternative has been selected, the next task is to put the potential solution into action. The plan should be implemented and, if necessary, refined and tried again.

The sixth step is to survey the outcome. After trying out the plan, the next step is to evaluate it. How did it go? Did it produce the desired outcome? If it has, then the problem is resolved. If the conflict has not been resolved, then you can start again at the third step (L) and start trying to list the alternatives again.

Assertiveness Skills

Assertiveness is an important skill because it is important to be able to express preferences, rights, needs, and desires in a way that is both considerate of one's own self-respect and the dignity of other people. Assertiveness is when you are neither passive (when you let yourself ignore your own dignity to be ignored by another person) nor aggressive (when a person's interactions disrespect others).

Assertiveness is composed of both nonverbal and verbal behaviors. In nonverbal behaviors, it is useful to strengthen smiles, relaxed posture, hand gestures, eye contact, and other nonverbal behaviors that convey attentiveness. On the other hand, it is useful to weaken things that indicate anxiety such as fidgeting or trembling, or uncomfortable eye contact, and overly intimidating postures or behavior.

In terms of verbal behaviors, there are many different things to think about.

To strengthen:
- *Features of speech*: confident tone, calmness, use of appropriate inflection, talking time, smooth and relaxed flow of speech
- *Content of speech*: using summaries of what other people say, using clear descriptions, saying no, asking for change in a way that conveys respect, seeking clarification, using I statements, expression of own views, protests at unfair treatment, negotiation, compromise, direct questions to others about their personal experience, statements to convey concern for others, compliments, positive toned statements, honesty.

To weaken:
- *Features of speech:* pauses, lowering volume at the end of sentences, mumbling, whining, yelling, raising voice
- *Content of speech:* praising yourself while putting others down, threats, put-downs,

accusations, judgments and criticisms, mind-reading statements, inappropriate self-disclosures that are way too intimate for the relations, self-deprecation, statements that indicate that someone else's needs are more important than your own.

Being properly assertive involves balancing speaking and listening. You need to be able to communicate what you need, while respecting that other people are individuals with needs. This involves both the ability to communicate what you want and to listen to what other people want.

When you are asking for things to be different, it is useful to ask for as specific change as possible. Requests are more effective when they are clear, concise, and based directly off of external behaviors. Instead of asking someone to be less of a slob, you should ask them to pick up the clothes off the floor. The request should be balanced and take seriously that the other person has needs and desires, too. It should also be consistent with the level of intimacy already present in the relationship.

When you propose something, then you have to listen and compromise about what the eventual solution is. Make sure to take seriously what other people are suggesting. And, when they do what you would like, compliment them and communicate that you are grateful they took your request seriously.

Chapter 13: Using Exposure to Counter Fear

Intense fear and anxiety can cause lots of problems in your life. Anxiety disorders are one of the most common things that people seek help for and they occur in up to one third of the general population. About 28% of the population will have a panic attack at one point in their life.

One of the best ways to deal with fear and anxiety is exposure therapy. Exposure is a targeted way to increase your familiarity with the things that cause you anxiety and help you deal with your emotions in a more appropriate way.

The basic structure of exposure therapy is focused around *desensitization*, which means exposing you to the thing that you fear in a systematic way. The goal is to push yourself to deal with the anxiety-provoking thing in progressive way. One aspect of this is to use your imagination and think about the anxiety producing thing while you are relaxed.

The goal is to replace the tension that you normally experience in response to the anxiety-producing thing with relaxation. While you think of the thing that causes yourself anxiety, engage in behaviors that relax you such as breathing and consciously relaxing your muscles. You could do things like thinking about the thing that causes you anxiety while you take a bath or otherwise do something that you enjoy.

While thinking about the thing that causes you anxiety could help, it is even more helpful to deal with the thing directly in person. People can be afraid of all sorts of things, from spiders and snakes, toilets or knives, or events, places, and situations. People can even be afraid of internal experiences, such as memories or emotions. When you are repeatedly exposed to something that you fear, the intensity of the emotional response often declines.

If you are afraid of spiders, for instance, the more you see spiders, the less that you may be afraid. Especially if you make a conscious effort to engage with the spiders and reach out to them, you will be able to increase the range of emotional responses to the spider. Instead of just responding with fear, eventually you may be able to respond with curiosity or interest. You may even get to a point where you can carefully remove the spider from the house where you might have previously run away.

A key part of exposure is that you do behaviors that are the normal ones that are provoked by fear or anxiety. If you prevent the typical behaviors associated with emotion and do things that are inconsistent with your emotion, you might eventually reduce the power that the emotion has over you. For instance, if you are afraid of public speaking, you might want to give a speech in front of a small group of people and consciously exhibit behaviors which are the opposite of your instincts. While you may want to look away, instead make eye contact. While you might want to shrink into yourself, adopt a confident posture and express enthusiasm about the topic of the speech. Do not allow yourself to engage in behaviors that are consistent with anxiety, because that will reinforce the emotions in your mind.

To talk about this process in more detail, let's start with the first step: assessment. In order to do exposure therapy, you need a clear sense of what the problem is. What exactly is the thing that you fear? Characterize it in as much detail as you can manage.

In addition to having a clear and specific sense of what you fear, it is important to have a precise understanding of your own emotional reaction. How intensely do you fear the object? How frequently does it happen? How long does it last? In addition to analyzing the emotions, it is also worth taking time to analyze any other manifestation of the fear. How does it affect your body? What thoughts do you have about the object of your fear?

Perhaps most importantly, you must clarify what types of behaviors that you engage in to respond to this fear. How do you avoid the fear and what are your behaviors that you use to self-soothe? What are the implications of these behaviors? What effects does this have on your life? Be aware of behaviors both big and small. They could be things like drinking or literally running away. They could be subtler, like fidgeting or skin-picking. Even just averting your eyes is a behavior of avoidance. These are the behaviors that you need to consciously avoid in the exposure process.

Being specific is really important. You may be afraid of public speaking in front of strangers, but not in front of friends and family. It could be the reverse!

You can be able to eat in public in some contexts, but not others. Some types of school work could make you afraid, but not others. You need to know exactly what you fear in order to begin to work on it. In general, self-knowledge is crucial in any process of self-change.

There are several types of exposure and we will now go through them one by one.

Imagination

This type of exposure uses the power of your imagination to help you develop positive associations to feared situations. This approach is best used when it is difficult or impossible to actually recreate the relevant situation or as a precursor to work up to exposure in life. It can also be a method to develop coping skills. For someone who fears job interviews, they might imagine a job interview and use that to practice different questions or explaining tough parts of her resume.

One form of exposure using your imagination is called *prolonged exposure* and it is typically used in the treatments for PTSD. If you do this on your own, do it carefully and with a mind to your own safety. It would be useful to have a trusted person be with you while you engage in this type of exposure. The way it works is to imagine and describe a specific traumatic event in detail. Imagine the sights, sounds, smells, and the things you touched. The goal of this is to demonstrate that while it is not pleasant to remember the trauma, you will not be in fact harmed by the memories. The traumatic event may have been dangerous, but the memories are not. By remembering the event, you will learn new associations. Instead of feeling in danger, you will just feel unpleasant.

Exposure in Life

When you expose yourself to the thing you fear in real life, it is an effective form of exposure. It can either be in your own home or out in the world. If you are afraid of heights, you may go up to high levels of parking garages, eating on the porch of a restaurant on the fifth floor, and walking across a high bridge. If you are afraid of contamination like dirt or germs, it could involve touching door knobs, sitting down on the floor, sitting on a public toilet seat, or other behavior without engaging in cleaning behaviors.

If you have social anxiety, this may involve getting into social situations such as parties, public speaking, or engaging in a group setting.

Sensation Exposure

This form of exposure is used for people who are afraid of bodily sensations. Someone might be afraid of minor chest pains, interpreting them as a major heart attack. Or it could be being afraid of a quickly beating heart.

In these cases, it is useful to provoke versions of these sensations that are harmless. If you are afraid of a quickly beating heart, you can engage in brief periods of intense exercise. If you are afraid of dizziness, you can spin around in circles.

Some people find themselves afraid of strong emotions. In that case, it can be useful to focus on the bodily sensations associated with the emotion and to direct your attention toward that. If you are afraid of feeling intense things, work yourself up physical and practice dealing with that way. Alternately, watch intense movies or read intense books. Learn to deal with emotions in a healthy way.

Opposite Action

This skill is one of the most important in exposure therapy. The skill of opposite action is learning to do the thing that is opposite what you feel like doing. Fear is frequently accompanied by the desire to flee; anger is accompanied by the urge to yell; shame is accompanied by the urge to hide. In all of those cases, opposite action would ask you to do the opposite thing that is felt. In the case of fear, move toward the thing as opposed to away from it. If you are socially anxious, you might have the desire to avoid attending a particular party. If you feel that, the idea would be to definitely attend the party and talk to as many people as possible. Opposite action is useful for many types of emotions, not just fear and anxiety, but is particularly useful in combating those. There are things that we have justifiable fear of, but most things that provoke anxiety in modern life aren't as scary as we treat them. Opposite action asks us to embrace that and to lean in to the fear.

Pacing Exposure

Once you have decided to do exposure, the next question is how to pace it. A common strategy is known as *graduated exposure*. This is exposing yourself to increasingly difficult and distressing things. If you are afraid of heights, it is about going increasingly higher. Maybe you start with watching videos of people rock climbing. Next, you look out a second-floor window. Next, you drive over a high bridge. Next, you walk over that bridge. Last, you stand at a high level in a parking garage and look down.

A different method for pacing exposure would be *flooding*. This means exposing yourself to the highest levels right at the beginning, starting with the most distressing elements. Flooding, counter-intuitively, has been shown to be very effective precisely because it provokes more fear. High levels of fear without negative outcomes is part of the point of exposure therapy.

You may feel too afraid to start off with the hardest types of exposure. That's okay. Start small and work your way up. If anything seems too scary, make a commitment to start with the smallest thing that provokes the fear response. Think about all the harm that your fear and anxiety cause in your life. Wouldn't it be nice not to have it? Focus on the dream of living without anxiety.

Eliminate Safety Signals

Safety signals are things in the environment which indicate that there is nothing to be afraid of. These, counter-intuitively, reduce the effectiveness of exposure. Things that can be safety signals include the presence of someone you trust, people giving you reassurance, or inanimate objects that act to reduce the fear, ranging from a magic charm to a cell phone.

The problem with these safety signals is that you may learn that things are okay if you have the safety signals. If someone is telling you over and over that you are okay, that mitigates the fear response and prevents you from learning that you are actually okay.

Sometimes people who have anxiety have rituals that they use to keep safe. They could be things like repeatedly checking the door, or verbalizing religious prayers, or touching things in a certain sequence. If you are engaging with exposure, you should try to cut back on these behaviors, because they will limit the benefits of exposure.

Conclusion

Thank you for making it through to the end of *Cognitive Behavioral Therapy: Changing Your Own Mind*, let's hope it was informative and able to provide you with all of the tools you need to achieve your goals whatever they may be.

The next step is to practice the skills that we have talked about in this book and to continue working on changing your own mind. You have the power to make yourself feel better, through working on cognitive and behavioral interventions. You can learn to deal with anything that faces you.

If you work on using these skills diligently and find that you still need help, seek out at a therapist that is trained in CBT to help you. Sometimes an outside perspective or voice is necessary to help you get the perspective you need on what is going on in your own mind.

Remember, if you feel that you are in danger of hurting yourself, you have to reach out. There are many people that can help you. Look into the suicide hotline in your country or reach out to emergency services. There is always a chance for your life to get better, remember that.

Finally, if you found this book useful in any way, a review is always appreciated!

Description

Cognitive behavioral therapy can change your life. CBT is the most researched type of therapy and scientists have found that it can be very effective in helping people with all kinds of mental health concerns. Whether you deal with depression, anxiety, eating disorders, personality disorders, bipolar disorder, PTSD – all of these things and more can be helped by CBT.

The secret is that our thoughts and judgments are what determines our perceptions of the world. The way we act and feel is a combination of the situations that happen to us and our judgments about those situations. By changing your thoughts, you can change how you feel.

The power to change your life is within your own mind. This book will teach you how to observe your thoughts and change them. It will give you the tools you need to make real, meaningful change, right away.

In addition to cognitive interventions, this book also talks about ways you can learn to problem solve and deal with specific issues in your life. Sometimes things seem unsurmountable, but when we look closer at them, we can learn ways to deal with what troubles us.

Regardless of what you struggle with, a better life is possible. All you need to do is take the first step toward helping yourself: buying this book. With this book, you can start a journey toward self-acceptance and self-love that can make you feel better each and every day.

- Learn the background of cognitive behavioral therapy and what makes it unique and special.
- Develop an understanding of the way your mind works. Learn the way that thoughts help determine your emotions and behaviors.
- Explore the "four factor model" of behavior, which is a tool that will help you change your life.
- Track the automatic thoughts that cause you pain and lead to behaviors that you regret.
- Learn to change your thoughts and make them more accurate and beneficial to the things you want to do in life.
- Track cognitive distortions and learn to stop them in your own life.
- Regulate your emotions and tolerate distress, even in the worst situations.
- Learn to get stuff done even if you don't feel like it.
- Develop organizational skills and the ability to plan your life.
- Solve problems and develop skills of resilience
- Learn mindfulness and how to be in the present
- Improve your relationships with other people.
- Conquer your fears through exposure therapy
- And more!

www.ingramcontent.com/pod-product-compliance
Lightning Source LLC
Chambersburg PA
CBHW071716020426
42333CB00017B/2293